An edible memoir from the back roads
and beaches of the Yucatan

THE PAINTED FISH AND OTHER MAYAN FEASTS

BY SONJA LILLVIK

CUZAN PRESS

Carrboro NC

Published by

Cuzan Press
108 A Old Pittsboro Rd
Carrboro NC 27510
Orders@Cuzanpress.com

Library of Congress Control Number: 2009909186
ISBN: 978-0-9824674-0-4

Cover and interior design by Shannon Bodie, Lightbourne, Inc.
Cover copy by Writetoyourmarket.com

In memory of Don Susano

Mi suegro

ACKNOWLEDGMENTS

It is with gratitude in my heart that I would like to thank the numerous people who have supported me through the long journey of completing this work. First, with appreciation I thank Gretchen Whalen for her interest and expertise on the Maya and her constant encouragement that inspired me to stay the course. Pamela Rhodes and Michael Scolieri have lent me their generous support to my morale but also supplies, staff, ideas, photos, paintings. The Craige-Hoffman household has provided me with a beautiful setting for mini writing retreats. My brother, Carl Lillvik, and his family have honored my dream with trust and loyalty. Many friends have seen me through in countless ways: Linda Krause, Gail Greene, Katharine Whalen, Audrey Townsend, Carroll Lassiter, Phil and Vicki Campbell, Lily Bertram, Mimi and Bill Fain, Catherine Gray, David Miller, Margy Nelson, Mary Szasz, Spencer Mace, Ramsey Tracy, Joanne Godbout, Sandra Hanen, Cristina Roman, Maria DiGiano, Jackie Helvey, Jim Ernest, Katherine Walton, Rory Flood, my cousin, and the entire Rosso family, my cousins. The Lopez family, now my family, accepted me with patience and showed me their world. A special thank you goes to all the Mayan cooks that shared their unwritten recipes and techniques with me. Admiration and thanks go to Donna Nielson and Carol Amorosco whose expertise brought the recipes to fruition with inspiration and skill. Natalie Goldberg's books inspired me to write in the first place and her teachings keep me writing. I recognize, with affection, Armando Lopez Rosado as my muse and my partner. Lastly, the project would not have been resurrected and completed without the artistry, skill, and thorough understanding of Anna Woods that brought the manuscript and book to completion.

FOREWORD

This cookbook has been simmering for a long time. To my knowledge, based on more than thirty years of research related travel on the Yucatan Peninsula, this cookbook presents the most authentic source for Mayan recipes ever compiled. Almost all of these recipes have been handed down over many generations. I suspect that many of the dishes are pre-Columbian in origin.

This book's author, Sonja Lillvik, has made her home on the Yucatan Peninsula since 1983. She is an extraordinary woman who is uniquely qualified to author this cookbook. I first met Sonja in Punta Allen while updating my field notes on the lobster fishery along Mexico's Caribbean Shore. I'd dropped by to visit with Armando Lopez, a good friend who I'd stayed with some five years earlier while doing my doctoral dissertation fieldwork focused on marine resources. Armando introduced me to Sonja; we shared a meal of lobster head soup, drank cold beer, and talked for hours. I learned that Sonja was on "vacation" from her job as manager of a resort up the coast and that we had friends in common who had recommended that she come down to meet Armando to learn more about local culture.

That was twenty-five years ago. Since that first meeting Sonja and I have been good friends. In the late 1980's, I was the principal investigator for ten Earthwatch Expeditions focusing on the lobster fishery in Punta Allen. On just a verbal handshake (we were on separate boats pulled alongside each other) Sonja and

Armando agreed to host our research teams. By that next summer, when our first team arrived, Cuzan Guest House had materialized, with accommodations for some thirty team members. From that first night, exquisite local dishes regularly appeared from the most rudimentary kitchen that you can imagine. Over the course of three years, our team of Mexican and American scientists and research assistants were treated to many fine meals. There's the old saying that "an army runs on its stomach." Sonja's kitchen magic was performed night after night; the good food that streamed out of her kitchen kept us all looking forward to the evening meal, no matter how hard we worked during the day.

So for the last quarter century, as a regular guest at the Cuzan Guest House, I've probably tasted every dish that you can produce using this cookbook. If you truly want to reproduce fine Mayan dishes, then there is no better guidebook than this. Every recipe in this book is authentic and tested. Traditionally, many of these dishes were based on verbal instructions such as "a pinch of this, about this much of that." Over the years, Sonja has spent long hours as a participant-observer in kitchens all over the peninsula. She speaks the language, knows the culture, and gets the recipes right. This cookbook has been some twenty-five years in the making; follow these unique recipes and you will produce great tasting—and truly authentic—Mayan dishes.

Dr. David L. Miller

SUNY Distinguished Teaching Professor of Geography
Waterman, Parrothead, and Author of *The Complete Paddler*

CONTENTS

INTRODUCTION

In the Land Called Sian Ka'an

In the land known to the Mayas as Sian Ka'an, "where the sky is born," my husband, Armando, and I welcome a small but steady stream of intrepid guests from all over the world. For more than twenty years, we have taken great pleasure in introducing newcomers to the complex and satisfying flavors of the foods of the Yucatán Peninsula.

In the early days of Cuzan Guest House, meals were freshly caught lobster doused with garlic and lime or fish swathed in banana leaves and cooked over an open fire. We served this simple, delicious seafood with black beans, rice, and baskets of hot, freshly baked tortillas followed by a fresh fruit dessert. Today, we have not stopped serving these foods at the tables of the Cuzan dining *palapa* (thatch-roofed house), but our kitchen has expanded as we continue to add local delicacies.

Now, as then, relying on foods that are available to the local Maya people, our meals feature distinctive regional cooking, Cuzan style. As a truly slow-food culture, Maya style cooking uses only the freshest of ingredients, always grown locally. Though lard is traditionally included in many dishes, it is not used in the selection of recipes for this collection. These recipes provide a unique opportunity for those who enjoy eating—as well as for health-conscious cooks—to expand their menus and their palates.

Fusion food, Mayan style, incorporates the influence of Spanish, French, Lebanese, Cuban and Caribbean cuisines. This collection of recipes is adapted from the labors of family and friends who use no books or written recipes. I first recorded ingredients and amounts in kilos and grams. Later, I had two professional American cooks, Donna Nielson and Carol Amoruso, adapt and test all recipes in the United States giving them the American equivalents in pounds and ounces. Armando and I offer this recipe collection so that you can enjoy and share the pleasure of Maya home cooking and eating with others wherever you may be.

Cuzan Guest House is in the state of Quintana Roo, on the Yucatán Peninsula of Mexico. You will find us at the northern entrance to Ascension Bay in the small lobster fishing village of Javier Rojo Gomez, popularly known as Punta Allen, about a four-hour drive south of Cancún. The last thirty miles of the trip are over a narrow sand road with jungle and lagoon on the right and the Caribbean on the left. This beautiful area is part of the World Biosphere Reserve, Sian Ka'an, and is a UNESCO World Heritage Site.

IN THE BEGINNING

The Maya

Native Americans have been on the North American continent since the Ice Age, reaching the pinnacle of civilization on the land where I live. I find this exciting.

Today most Maya live in the same areas as their ancestors: southern Mexico, Belize, Guatemala and Honduras. Thirty or more Maya languages are still spoken. Although some modern Maya have opted for city life, most live in rural areas and maintain traditional customs and diet.

The ancient Maya kept a written history and developed a complex calendar based on accurate astronomical observations. Their number system included a symbol that functioned as zero. Their magnificent architecture continues to amaze and fascinate archeologists and tourists alike.

Pyramids, temples and ceremonial causeways, all built without metal tools, attest to the organizational engineering acumen of the ancient Maya. Advanced systems of mathematics and astronomy reveal abstract genius. The Maya developed technologies that allowed them to thrive

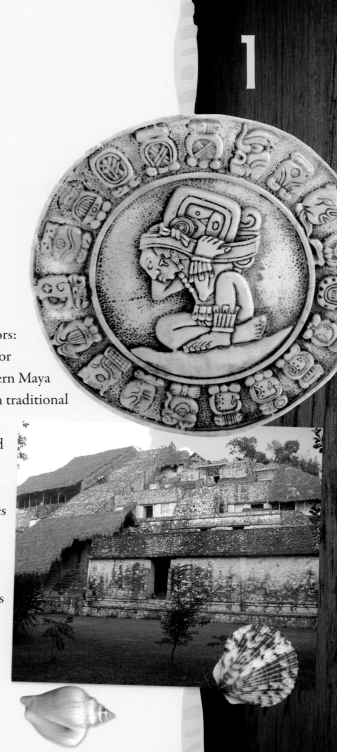

in a land of scarce soil and water. Reverence for food and water and practical wisdom characterize the Maya, from ancient times to the present. The same spirit that enabled these people to flourish on the land thousands of years ago graces the Maya kitchen today.

The Territory

Oftentimes when orienting a guest, I thrust out my open palmed hand to illustrate my lecture. The thumb extension, I explained, running my left index finger along the edges, represents the peninsula and the palm and fingers the rest of Mexico. Due to this geographical separation, the indigenous Maya were able to maintain distance from the central government for many years. There were even occasions when they asked to be part of the United States government and I think now how fortunate this did not take place—fortunate for me, as I never would have found my husband because he would be on a reservation. Instead, the Maya persevered and survived hacienda life and the Caste War as well as nefarious business deals with *henequen* and *chicle* exports.

Originally, the peninsula was one state, the Yucatán. Later, it was divided into three states: Campeche, Yucatán and Quintana Roo. The peninsula is sometimes referred to by locals as *tres hermanos*, or three brothers, as they raise a closed fist in solidarity to their common Maya heritage. All states have sizeable lateral borders of water of either the Gulf of Mexico to the north or the Caribbean Sea to the east. Therefore, seafood has always been a staple for coastal diets, complimented by jungle game on feast days.

Geographically cut off from the mainland by a narrow isthmus, much of the culture and language survived. After years of rapid change, new pride has emerged as young Maya speakers are now rewarded with scholarships for advanced education. These young people are from homes where Maya is the first language and Spanish, the second language, is sometimes not learned until school age. I, like many Maya people, learned Spanish as a second language, after my native English. Over the years, visitors from the interior of Mexico have teased me about my southern accent—in Spanish! "Oh," giggle, giggle, "You speak like a Yucateca," They say. I have been told this many times. However, I take it as a compliment because it means I have captured the singsong slow Maya influence on the Spanish of this region rather than the vowel-flattening accent I started with.

Ritual hammock time

BREAD OF LIFE, OR ZEN AND THE ART OF TORTILLA MAKING

2

Corn, "the sunshine of the gods," was central to the ancient Maya. In the form of *tortillas*, it appears in most Maya meals today. Tortilla making, like all bread making, requires practice, a light touch, and attention to detail. From mixing the masa to forming perfect spheres of dough and evenly pressing them into flat cakes, Maya women reveal patience and balance in this age-old art.

When I first arrived in the Yucatán, I did not even eat corn tortillas. However, I soon came to enjoy this nutritious, tasty bread when Felipa, the head cook where I worked, began offering her handmade tortillas to me hot off the *comal*, or griddle. Later, the second cook also offered me her delicate, perfectly formed tortillas when she prepared food for her family. The pride and care taken in the ritual-like making of fresh tortillas *a mano*, by hand, gave me a new appreciation for this basic food source.

Much later, I learned to pat the tortillas gently into shape. A friend, Elena, laughed as she cajoled and encouraged my early attempts. Like the ancient Maya, Elena still soaks whole kernels of corn in water and lime or calcium oxide, cooks them slowly on an open fire, and then grinds them to make her daily tortillas.

Before understanding tortilla making, I offered to buy fresh tortillas from the tortilleria instead of having someone make them by hand. I soon learned that most Maya women want to make tortillas. Their day would be incomplete without this ritual.

Seated at a low, three-legged table near an open fire topped with a comal, the women of the household quietly share the task. The restful atmosphere that takes over the kitchen during tortilla making never ceases to amaze me. No one is harried or careless. Few words are spoken, but the women always distribute rolled up hot tortillas to the various children who inevitably gather around. It is a soothing time linking the day's meal with countless meals from past generations.

The perfectly shaped and uniformly sized tortillas are wrapped in colorful hand-embroidered cloth towels or placed gently in a *lech*, a hollowed out gourd with a quarter-inch thick wall that retains heat. Colorful napkin-lined baskets are a serving alternative. The generosity and friendliness of the cook is easily measured by the exquisite stacks of flawless tortillas.

In experiments with tortilla making, I found that almost anybody can form a tortilla in her (or his) own way. However, to form them repeatedly with deft fingers, in the gentle rhythmic patting characteristic of the Maya, takes practice and more practice. To me, it is a lifelong study, which requires calmness and patience. One of the compromises in my

The Painted Fish and Other Mayan Feasts

kitchen is to use a tortilla press initially and then pat the tortilla into its final form. This can shorten the tortilla making ritual by half. Also, unskilled laborers such as children, spouses and guests can be pressed into service, first to prepare the balls of dough and then to make the crude rounds.

One of the secrets I have learned is to moisten your fingertips ever so lightly with hot water to prevent sticking when making tortillas by hand. When cooking the tortilla, place it on the comal first with the cara, or face, down. When heated throughout and forming brown spots flip to the other side until heated. Flip again. Use a folded paper towel to press the tortilla in order to encourage it to inflate, the sign of a well-made tortilla.

You may not be able to cook on a comal over an open fire, but the joys of making and eating fresh tortillas can still be yours. If you are unable to make fresh tortillas, you can substitute store-bought ones, but you will lose all of the pleasure and much of the nutrition and flavor of those freshly made delicacies. Luckily, there are now many tortillerias in the United States and fresh, machine made tortillas are available or you can buy the uncooked masa to make tortillas at home.

Fresh corn tortillas are used primarily in making the soft tacos famous in the Yucatán. They are also used by the Maya as a utensil. A whole tortilla is folded in half, torn in two and each half torn into a triangle to make a scoop for black beans. Used open on the palm of your hand, a tortilla serves as a plate for juicy morsels. Rolled up with the palms of your hands, it is used to push your food onto your fork.

Bread of Life, or Zen and the Art of Tortilla-Making

11

TORTILLA DE MAIZ— CORN TORTILLA RECIPES

Tortillas Handmade the Yucatecan Way

The Maya believe that man was created from corn. Yum Kaax, the Maya corn god, is honored daily at dawn. In the Yucatán Peninsula folks have stacks of piping hot fragrant orbs of handmade corn tortillas illuminating the breakfast table by 7:30. So, beware of well-intended instructions on the packages of masa harina and take the extra time to turn out pliant light tortillas. You will need a tortilla press for best results, or you can head down to the Yucatán and study with those remaining señoras who press tortillas out with their fingers.

Ingredients:
2 cups fresh masa or masa harina:
     Maseca, Minsa, or Quaker Brand
1 ⅛ cup warm water, or as directed on
     the bag

Preparation:
    Combine the masa flour and warm water in a large bowl. Mix well with your hands for about 5 minutes to form a firm ball, adding more water if necessary and leave to rest for thirty minutes. Divide the dough into 16 pieces and roll into balls. Cover with a damp cloth or plastic wrap to keep from drying out. Heat a heavy ungreased griddle or comal over a medium flame.

Made with a Press

Have ready two squares of plastic wrap, as from a food storage bag, large enough to cover the plate of your tortilla press. Place one round of dough a little off center toward the hinge and flatten it slightly. Place the second plastic square over the dough and gently lower the upper plate of the press, pressing down lightly but firmly with the handle to flatten the tortilla to a little more than ⅛ inch. Open the press and turn the tortilla in the plastic halfway around. Repeat the pressing, keeping the tortilla at just over ⅛-inch thickness. Open.

Gently peel the top sheet of plastic off the tortilla, invert the tortilla onto the palm of your hand and take off the other layer of plastic. Place the tortilla flat onto the heated griddle or comal and cook for about 30 seconds or until the edges begin to come away from the pan. Turn the tortilla over with the fingers or a spatula and cook for another 20–30 seconds, or until the underside begins to show light brown spots. Now turn the tortilla a second time, onto its original cooking side, and let this side lightly brown, too. You should see the tortilla puff up in the center. It will deflate on its own as it cools. Remove the tortilla from the heat and put into a cloth lined basked. As the tortillas are made, stack them in the basket, keeping them covered so that they stay warm and soft. Makes 16 tortillas 4 inches in diameter.

Hand Made

To try your hand at the Maya way: Cut two sheets of plastic from a food storage bag 5 by 5 inches. Place one sheet of plastic on a smooth surface. Form your sphere of dough, and place it in the center of the plastic. Begin pressing lightly with the fingertips, working the dough outwards into an even circle while turning and guiding with your other hand until the dough is approximately ⅛ inch thick. Remove from the plastic and cook as described previously.

You may be wondering how the señoras did this before plastic bags. The answer is simple: they used pieces of banana leaves freshly plucked from the yard, warmed and cut to size.

Very deft Maya women form their tortillas as they rotate the masa, almost as if on a clay wheel, their left hand placed on its side, curved to form an even arc, their right hand rotating the tortilla on the plastic while tamping it outwards with their fingertips into the right thickness. Makes 12–15 tortillas, 4 to 5 inches in diameter.

Tostaditas

Ingredients:

    1 doz. day old corn tortillas
    2 pints cold water
    1 tbsp. salt
    Oil for frying

Preparation:

    Stack the tortillas, 3 or 4 at a time, and cut into 6 pie-shaped pieces. They need to be cut before they dry out too much, but the drier they are, the less oil they will absorb when you cook them. Dissolve the salt in the water in a good-sized bowl. Separate the tortilla pieces then drop them by handfuls into the salted water, swish them around, and put them into a colander to drain. Heat the oil to a depth of ½ inch in a heavy frying pan until hot. Add the tortilla pieces, a few at a time, turning with tongs until they are crisp and golden brown.

    Remove to paper toweling. Add more oil to the pan as necessary, letting it heat up each time before continuing. Makes 6 dozen.

    Store in an airtight container. The *tostadas* can be reheated on a cookie sheet in a moderate oven for 5 minutes.

Don Nacho with Feliciana

Tortillas-Waj

Nacho, an excellent cook and local storyteller, told me that this unique tortilla/egg dish evolved when the whole family worked the *milpa*, a subsistence farm where families grew such things as corn, beans, sweet potatoes, and squash. The milpa could be a few kilometers from the house and changed location from year to year due to the traditional slash and burn technique in which a section of the jungle was cut, cleared and burned. After the ash partially dissolved with the first rains of spring, the Maya men would walk the land with a lean stick, poking holes in the ground and planting corn kernels, which they carried in a *sabucan* (bag) over their shoulders.

While the parents and older children were gone on their journeys to the milpa, smaller children stayed at home with their grandparents.

During the early morning tortilla ritual, the grandmother slowly made tortillas in the dirt floor palapa, which is a thatched roof house. Then, when she heard a cackle in the bushes, the grandmother would send a child out to find and retrieve the newly laid egg. She broke the egg and slipped it into a slightly slit, freshly made, partially cooked corn tortilla that was gently replaced on the fire to finish cooking. It was served with chiltomate salsa to the finder of the egg, while the rest of the children strained to hear another cackle.

Pimes

Pimes, also called *Gordas* or fat tortillas, are larger, robust versions of the delicate hand made tortillas and are simple to make. Men seem to favor this style of tortilla when they cook. At Rancho el Angel, Don Jose, the caretaker, prepares hefty tortillas eliminating the need for making huge quantities. With tortilla dough, make thick, 6-inches-wide tortillas and cook them. (Add cooked beans to the masa to create an even more nutritious appetizer.) Top with either Xnipek or onion and cilantro or your favorite topping of your own invention.

Ingredients:
   1 ¼ cups masa harina
   ¾ cup water

Preparation:
   Mix the masa harina and the water to make soft dough as described in the corn tortilla recipe or use fresh masa. Heat a comal or griddle until medium hot. Divide the dough into 8 pieces. Working on a heavy square of plastic wrap, roll pieces into balls and flatten with the heel of your palm. Then press out evenly with your fingertips to make ¼-inch thick rounds. Cook for about 2 minutes on each side until crispy and slightly browned. Makes 8.

Tortillas de Harina—Flour Tortillas
Relatively speaking, flour tortillas are a modern invention. Although they are much less nutritious than the corn variety, they are more familiar in the American diet, with its refined white flour. Flour tortillas have been introduced to the Yucatán from the North and are used to accompany specific dishes for a holiday or as a festive treat.

Comadre's Flour Tortillas

Some cooks specialize in making rich flour tortillas. One of these is a woman who has been called "Comadre" for so long that her real name is nearly forgotten. Here is her basic flour tortilla recipe.

Ingredients:

2 cups all purpose flour
1 tsp. baking powder
½ tsp. salt
2 tbsp. vegetable shortening
⅔ cup water

Preparation:

Place the flour, baking powder and salt in a large bowl. Rub the shortening in with your fingertips until it is well blended with the flour. Add ⅔ cup warm water and work the dough with your hands for a minute or two. The dough should hold together well—add small amounts of water gradually if too dry, or additional sprinklings of flour if too moist. Knead by hand on a lightly floured surface or with a dough hook in the bowl for about 5 minutes until the dough is smooth and elastic.

Divide the dough into 10 pieces and roll each piece into a ball. Cover the balls with a damp cloth or plastic wrap and set aside. Heat an ungreased comal or griddle to medium hot.

Take one of the balls, leaving the rest covered, and press it out on a lightly floured surface to about ½-inch thick. Now with a rolling pin roll it out into a round about 6 inches in diameter. Carefully lift the tortilla with both hands and place on the heated comal.

Let it cook for about a minute until the dough becomes opaque and light brown spots begin to appear on the underside. Turn once to lightly brown the other side. Remove the tortilla to a heavy towel and wrap until the remaining tortillas are completed. Repeat for each tortilla. Makes 10 tortillas.

Capi's Flour Tortilla with Coconut Milk

For a subtle, delicate change in flavor, I highly recommend the following recipe taught to me by an older male friend, Don Jose Canto of Cozumel. He is well known on the Caribbean coast as a worthy sea captain and *copra* (coconut) rancher. His kitchen is well stocked and highly organized, just as one would expect of a ship's captain.

Capi, as Don Jose is known to many, personally prepares these yummy tortillas using a small rolling pin to shape them. At

Capi's Kitchen

his remote ranch, I have delighted in many savory meals that included these delicious flour tortillas made with coconut milk. (Also, see our section on making coconut milk.) Capi's style of tortilla making is well worth the work.

Ingredients:
2 cups all purpose flour
2 tsp. baking powder
½ tsp. salt
3 tbsp. vegetable shortening
⅔ cup coconut milk

Preparation:
Place the flour, baking powder and salt in a large bowl. Cut the shortening into the mixture, and then crumble with the fingers until it is well blended. Add the coconut milk and work into dough with the hands for a minute or two. The dough should be moist and elastic, not crumbly. Add small amounts of water gradually if too dry, or additional sprinklings of flour if too moist. Knead by hand on a lightly floured surface or with a dough hook in the bowl for about 5 minutes until the dough is smooth and elastic. Divide the dough into 10 pieces and roll each piece into a ball. Cover the balls with a damp cloth or plastic wrap and set aside.

Continue as for the tortillas de Harina: heat an ungreased comal or griddle to medium hot. Take one of the balls, leaving the rest covered, and press it out on a lightly floured surface to about ½ inch thick. Now roll it out into a round about 6 inches in diameter. Carefully lift the tortilla with both hands and place on the heated comal.

Let it cook for about a minute until the dough becomes opaque and light brown spots begin to appear on the underside. Turn once and lightly brown the other side. Remove the cooked tortilla to a cloth napkin and wrap. Makes 10.

Fried Flour Tortillas

Fried flour tortillas are seen more often in northern Mexico, but I mention them here so that you will not discard any leftover flour tortillas. Fry your day-old tortillas and store them in an airtight container. They are excellent with dips and sauces.

Flour Tortillas de Don Vic

From Don Vic, an old gentleman on the coast, I learned an unusual way to make a sweet tortilla. When you add egg and a little sugar to the flour, the tortilla is more cake-like; though it is still cooked on the griddle. This is fine bread for brunch.

Don Vic worked for Capi at the coconut ranch. He was always very generous with his light, sweet tortillas and coffee. He cooked on the top of a steel drum that had a section cut out (see illustration). The drum was filled with sand to the level of the cutout, and coconut husks were burned on the sand to heat the top of the drum. This style of oven is often used all along the coast. Your griddle or frying pan will do just fine, too.

3

THE SPICE OF LIFE: CHILES

The Land of the Habanero

In a Yucatecan village, a dooryard garden surrounds each home. Here grow radishes, tomatoes and a variety of *chiles*. Cilantro, *epazote*, and *yerba buena* flourish in raised troughs made from dug-out tree trunks, out of reach of the chickens. Orange, *limón*, and avocado trees offer shade as well as fruit, while the *jícara* tree provides the family's bowls.

Once when I drove to the Yucatán peninsula from the U.S., the officials at the Mexican border and the following customs check asked me where I was going. When I told them I was going to Yucatán, they responded, "Si, Si, the land of the Habanero." By then I had been living in the land of the Habanero for several years and had learned to appreciate the hottest chile pepper in the world. Now Habanero chiles are exported to the U.S. and even grown there; they can easily be found in supermarkets. As for the name, one theory suggests that the Habanero originally came from Havana, Cuba. A variety of chocolate-colored Habanero is referred to as "Cubanos." At one time, Habaneros were primarily grown in the Yucatán or in the West Indies. Now hot foods are a popular trend, and Habanero is produced all over the world. Homegrown chiles of various kinds appear on menus throughout the U.S. Since chiles cross-fertilize easily, their pollen carried by the wind, there are over 100 varieties, including some new flavors. Now, many brands of bottled Habanero can be found or special-ordered at your grocer. My favorite combines Habanero with sweet potatoes and is called Flounder Juice.

The heat in all chiles is in the oil, capsaicin, that is especially concentrated in the seeds, veins, and flesh closest to the stem. Habaneros change color from green to orange to red as they ripen and increase in hotness. They culminate in a fiery heat, but with a distinctive flavor that leans toward citrus.

Yucatecans enjoy this deliciously fiery pepper every day. Capsicum pollution is common here. In Maya villages, Habaneros are often dried, roasted and ground in to a powder. Sometimes so much acrid smoke is in the air that when I step out on my third floor balcony I immediately feel an irritation in my throat followed by coughing and teary eyes as well as my hasty retreat indoors.

When I first practiced Maya hospitality here on the coast, I felt a strong responsibility to educate (or perhaps warn) visitors about the fiery Habaneros that are so characteristic of this area and its cuisine. On the other hand, Armando likes to pick Cubanos from his personal crop, remove the stems, and place three or four in the palm of his hand. Then he casually offers them to me or some other unsuspecting person as *caramelos* (caramels) and laughs.

The Painted Fish and Other Mayan Feasts

Using Habaneros will introduce your friends and family to the different Yucatecan flavors of "hot" and "hotter." To prepare the walnut-sized peppers, you dice them finely. When cutting hot chiles either hold them only by the stem or use a fork rather than your hands. You can also use rubber gloves to protect your fingers. The oils from Habaneros mix readily with the oils from the skin. Hands that have handled Habaneros can burn the eyes and other sensitive parts of the body very painfully. Habaneros should carry a warning: "Do not touch your eyes!"

For best results, follow this advice:

1. Use discretion (always taste a salsa for heat before using it).

2. If you eat a chile that is too hot for you, DO NOT reach for water or cold beer. It will only make matters worse. Instead, eat a teaspoon or more of sugar, savoring it in your mouth, if sugar is not available try chewing a bit of tortilla or a piece of bread.

3. The real *MAYA SECRETO*: If you or one of your kitchen mates makes the serious mistake of touching the eyes when handling chiles, there is a secret solution. Take a hank of hair, yours or anothers, roll it around your finger and pat the eye. Be sure to hold the hair so the ends do not touch the eye (this would not feel too good). Continue patting lightly several times and release. Blink back to normal, sting free sight—truly amazing! The natural oils from the hair help dilute the stinging Habanero oils. Water will not wash the oil away.

CHILES: TYPES AND INTENSITIES

Habanero

Chiles add heat and flavor to most Yucatec Maya foods. Besides being a great source of vitamin C, this lantern shaped chile throws a major party for the mouth and taste buds. Often even seasoned chile eaters are seen panting with eyes tearing after biting into a Habanero. This "rush" from chiles sends endorphins to the brain and explains why many folks seem to be addicted to the fiery taste. In hot weather, the sweat chile provokes helps to cool the body after the initial "hit." Drying and pulverizing chiles brings out the *picante*, or hot, flavors even more.

Chile Xcatik—Blond Chile in Maya

A long pale yellow, green or red, thick-skinned chile is less fiery but very flavorful. It can be used whole or whole with a slit to let its flavor merge when placed on top of a stew. Later, it is removed and served on a separate plate

for all the diners to pat with their tortillas to add punch to the taste. Sometimes it is char roasted and used the same way or in *escabeche*. A banana pepper can be your substitute.

Chile Seco

This young green chile turns to a rich red when mature. When toasted or flamed it turns to a distinctive burnt or charcoal brown color and is later ground and used for sauces like *recado negro*. Very potent!

Chile de Arbol—Tree Chile

Despite its name, this bright red (when mature) chile actually grows on a hearty leggy bush.

The fruit itself is thin and two to three inches long. Rarely used whole, it is dried in the sun, toasted and ground to a fine reddish orange powder and then stored. Combined with salt, it is used on fresh fruit and vegetables like jícama, cucumber, mangoes and citrus.

Chile Jalapeño

Though not of the region, and mostly found pickled in cans, Jalapeño has been adopted by the local population for use in escabeche and salads. Jalepeño is thick skinned and green in color.

Chile Serrano

Dark green and less hot than the local varieties of chile, Serranos are cultivated in the mountains of Mexico. They are fleshy and eaten raw or roasted.

Chile Guajillo

This large, wide, almost six-inch long, deep red chile is dried and brought to the peninsula from the interior. It has a thin skin and is more sharply flavorful giving sauces like escabeche a rich taste rather than picante or hot.

Chile Poblano

Poblanos are dark green about the size of a bell pepper and taper to a point. They have a pleasant and distinctive flavor and can be found fresh, dried and canned. They are not known to be hot, but can be. They are used for *chile relleno* (stuffed peppers) by removing stems and veins and soaking in cold salted water.

Chile Ancho

Known more for flavor than bite, chile Ancho is a dark dried Poblano chile used in stews and sauces for complexity in flavor.

RECADOS, SALSAS AND SAUCES

RECADOS

Recados are spice pastes that are diluted in soups and stews or are rubbed onto meat, fish or poultry. When Carol Amuroso, who helped adapt these recipes, first learned of recados, she was excited as she realized they resemble India's curry pastes, of which she is an aficionado. She eagerly tested these recipes, toasting spices to bring out flavors and then grinding them together in a *metate* or mortar and pestle. Locals usually make a big batch and preserve the paste for future daily use. Recados are made fresh or they can be bought from a specialist in recados. They are now available in many supermarkets and specialty stores. They are used almost daily in making either a red, black or a white sauce.

Achiote pods

Achiote

I first came upon this savory spice in its natural state. My sister-in-law, Emma, snapped a dark round spring pod from the lipstick tree growing in her yard—then another and another. We returned to the kitchen with our hands full, carefully holding the unusual pods. We opened them and gently squeezed the thin layer of skin and juice from the many seeds inside, leaving our fingers as bright red as the marinade produced from the ground seed.

Achiote or annatto seeds come from a small tropical tree that grows spiny pods among its delicate white or pale pink flowers. A hard reddish pulp is removed by steeping in hot lard or oil that is later strained. The orange colored and flavored oil is used for poultry,

beef, pork and fish. A paste called *recado rojo* is a blend of whole ground achiote seeds and other spices. The paste is diluted with citrus juice and used as a marinade on just about anything. I call it the "Maya barbecue sauce." It is the sauce often used in the *pibil* methods of Maya cooking.

You do not have to go on vacation to find achiote. It is now available in specialty stores, blended into a paste and neatly packaged. A friend of mine likes it so much that she uses it in her scrambled eggs. Use lime juice to dilute the paste to make a marinade. Or, mix it with water and use to paint your face (as the Maya Chieftains did) to celebrate Halloween or Carnival.

Pibil is a Maya method of cooking in a pit of hot coals. Dishes previously cooked in an earth oven are called pibil as in *pollo pibil* and *cochinita pibil*. These can be cooked in covered pots or modern ovens.

Recado Rojo

Ingredients:
>   4 tbsp. achiote
>   1 stick cinnamon stick crushed (if you're
>   not using Mexican cinnamon,
>   use only half)
>   10 whole cloves
>   1 tbsp. black peppercorns
>   Pinch whole cumin
>   2 tsp. dried oregano
>   4 cloves garlic
>   1 tbsp. oil

Preparation:
>   Put the spices in a spice grinder and grind to a fine powder. Turn out into a small bowl. Put the garlic through a press into the bowl and add the oil to make a paste.

Recado Negro

Ingredients:
>   1 dried Guajillo chile, stemmed, seeded
>   and deveined

Recado Rojo

1 dried Ancho chile, stemmed, seeded
     and deveined
1 dried chile Arbol, stemmed, seeded
     and deveined
2 tbsp. oregano, pan toasted
1 whole cinnamon stick, crushed
     (if you're not using Mexican
     cinnamon, use only half)
1 tbsp. whole black peppercorns
1 tbsp. salt
2 cloves garlic
2 tbsp. white onion, minced
1 tbsp. oil
2 tbsp. white vinegar
Dash of Tabasco, or other hot red chile
     sauce.

Heat a comal or flat pan over medium heat. Tear the chiles into flat pieces and place the pieces on the comal, pressing them flat to the surface. Toast the chiles, turning them over occasionally to keep them from charring, until they are crisp and break at the touch. Remove from the heat, break into bits, and place in a spice grinder together with the oregano, cinnamon, cumin seeds, pepper, and salt and grind to a powder. Sauté the onion and garlic in the oil until very soft but not browned. Sift the spices through a fine strainer into a mortar. Add the garlic and onion, vinegar, dash of tabasco and pound to a paste. You can also use a small bowl and strong wooden spoon, pressing on the mixture with the back of the spoon to make a paste. Makes about ½ cup.

Recado Para Escabeche

Ingredients:

1 tbsp. pan toasted oregano
1 cinnamon stick, crushed (if you are
      not using Mexican cinnamon,
      use a 1-inch piece)
4 allspice berries
4 whole cloves
1 tsp. whole peppercorns
2 tsp. salt

2 cloves garlic
1 tbsp. white vinegar
1 tbsp. oil

Preparation:

Grind the oregano, cinnamon, allspice berries, whole cloves, salt and peppercorns to a fine powder in a spice grinder or a mortar. Strain through a fine mesh into in a small bowl. Put the garlic cloves through a press into the bowl. Stir in the vinegar and oil to make a paste. Makes ¼ cup.

SALSAS

Salsa, Americanized from the Spanish, is now practically a household word. It is available freshly ready-made as well as jarred or canned and though flavorful, nothing compares to making your own. Salsas are adaptable to personal tastes and color aesthetic, and can be based on what you have on hand in your kitchen. Do not hesitate to experiment. Salsas accompany all meals. If a salsa is not present it is because one whole chile is available to be bitten into (only for the intrepid chile eater), or to give the appropriate fire a chile can be sliced or shredded at the tip for patting onto a tortilla an action called *chuch* in Maya. Sometimes tortillas and salsa alone are a fine snack, or you can include refried beans or avocados and you have lunch tacos.

Goddaughter, Deborah, with puppy, Mariposa

Salsa X-ni P'eek—Dog's Nose Salsa

This is the most common of salsas. It is colorful, easy to make, and it is available as *salsa fresca* (ready-made) in many supermarkets. I will let you determine the relationship between a dog's nose (the Maya name) and this perky salsa.

Ingredients:

1 cup finely chopped seeded tomato
½ cup finely chopped purple onion
½ cup cilantro leaves, coarsely chopped
1 chile Habanero, minced
½ cup bitter orange juice, or 6 tbsp. lime
    juice and 2 tbsp. orange juice
Salt to taste

Preparation:

Mix all the ingredients together and serve.

Salpicón—Spicy Radish Salsa

Bright red large bulbed radishes are displayed in markets and in front of beef stands selling the makings for *chocolomo*. *Salpicón* can be added to stews and soups for a tangy flavour.

Ingredients:

¼ cup red onion, minced
½ cup radishes, minced
2 tbsp. cilantro, minced
¼ cup sour orange or lime juice
Pinch of powdered chile Piquin or
    Cayenne chile to taste

Preparation:

Combine all the ingredients in a small bowl. Mix well and serve at room temperature. Makes about 1 cup.

Tomato Salsa in a Blender

This salsa is quick to make and retains a hearty red color. It can be used in a multitude of ways. Experiment.

Ingredients:

1 lb. plum tomatoes, boiled, peeled.
½ cup chopped onion
1 tsp. (or more) minced Habanero chile
2 tbsp. coarsely chopped cilantro

Preparation:

Blend the tomatoes, onion and chile briefly. Pour into a bowl and stir in the cilantro. Let stand for half an hour before serving. Makes about 2 cups.

Salsa Chiltomate I

When barbecuing, do not fail to make this richly-flavored salsa. Roast the tomatoes on an ungreased comal or cast iron griddle until the skin is well browned with a little charring. You can also use a good broiler for this, turning the tomatoes from time to time. Either peel the tomatoes, or just remove the charred patches. The browned skin gives a good flavor.

Roasting plum tomatoes

Ingredients:

4 plum tomatoes, roasted, seeded and chopped
1 medium white onion, roasted, peeled and chopped
1 Habanero chile, roasted, peeled, seeded and minced
1 small head garlic, roasted, the individual cloves peeled and chopped
2 tbsp. chopped cilantro

Preparation:

In a small bowl, combine all the ingredients, mash together to release flavors. Serve at room temperature with barbecued meat, chicken, lobster or other main entrée together with warm tortillas, beans and rice. Makes about 1 cup.

Salsa Chiltomate II

Ingredients:

    2 lbs. Roma tomatoes roasted, seeded
        and chopped
    ¼ cup olive oil
    ½ onion, chopped
    2 whole Habanero chiles
    Salt to taste

Preparation:

Blend the tomatoes for a few seconds to make a rough purée, or grind with a pestle in a mortar. Heat the oil in a skillet and sauté the onion until cooked but not browned. Add the tomato, whole chiles and salt and cook the mixture down to about 2 ½ cups. Remove the chiles and serve the salsa warm on the side.

Chiltomate Salsa

Habanero Chile Simple Salsa

Ingredients:

    2 Habanero chiles, seeded and minced
    3 tbsp. lime juice
    ½ tsp. salt

Preparation:

Mix and serve at room temperature as a means of spicing up any food. I often just spoon out some of the flavored lime juice and sprinkle it over food, leaving the chile behind in the dish. Makes ¼ cup

Mango Salsa

Springtime in Quintana Roo is time for mango mania. We eat and cook with mangos almost daily.

Ingredients:

    ½ cups peeled diced mango
    ½ cup seeded diced tomato
    ½ cup peeled, seeded chopped cucumber
    ¼ cup chopped red onion
    3 tbsp. lime juice
    2 tbsp. chopped cilantro
    1 tsp. (or more) minced Habanero
    ½ tsp. salt
    ¼ tsp. pepper

Preparation:

Mix in a small bowl and let stand half an hour. Makes about 3 cups.

Onion Salsa

Ingredients:

½ cup finely chopped red onion
½ to 1 chile Habanero, seeded and minced
2 tbsp. vinegar
Salt to taste

Preparation:

Combine ingredients and serve. Makes about ½ cup.

Cebolla Encurtida—Pickled Onions

Ingredients:

1 red or white onion cut lengthwise and
sliced into thin crescents
2 tbsp. white vinegar
½ tsp. salt

Preparation:

Place the onion slices in a bowl. Pour boiling water over to cover and let stand for a minute. Drain and mix with vinegar and salt. Marinate for an hour. Makes about 1 cup.

Cabbage Salsa

Salsa de Repollo—Cabbage Salsa

Though a versatile salsa, it is always used with kibis.

Ingredients:

1 cup finely shredded cabbage
2 tbsp. minced onion
2 Roma tomatoes, seeded and diced
2 tbsp. lime juice
Salt and pepper to taste

Preparation:

Mix all the ingredients together and let stand for 15 minutes to half an hour. Taste and add a few drops more lime juice and additional salt and pepper if needed. Serves 4 to 6.

Salsa de Piña—Pineapple Salsa

This is another great salsa using fresh fruit.

Ingredients:

2 cups finely chopped fresh pineapple
1 cup seeded chopped tomato
½ cup peeled seeded chopped cucumber
¼ cup chopped red onion
3 tbsp. chopped cilantro
3 tbsp. lime juice
2 cloves garlic, minced
1 tsp. brown sugar
1 tbsp. olive oil
½ tsp. salt
¼ tsp. pepper

Preparation:

Mix the ingredients together in a small bowl and let stand for an hour. Makes about 1 quart.

Tomatillo Salsa—Green Tomato Salsa

Ingredients:

1 lb. tomatillos, husks removed and rinsed
1 small onion, chopped
1 large clove garlic, chopped
1 tsp. (or more) Habanero chile, seeded and minced
2 tbsp. cilantro leaves
½ tsp. sugar
½ tsp. salt
1 small ripe avocado, peeled and diced (optional)

Preparation:

In a medium saucepan, cover the tomatillos with water. Bring to a boil, lower the heat, and simmer 3 minutes or until soft, but not mushy and breaking apart. Drain, reserving the liquid. Put all the ingredients in a blender and blend briefly until mixed. You can also put the ingredients in a bowl and mash thoroughly.

If the sauce is too thick, add some of the cooking liquid. This sauce will keep well for a few days. Makes about 3 cups.

Note: Canned tomatillos can also be used. Drain them and use water to dilute the salsa.

Salsa Tamulado—Mashed Salsa

Ingredients:

2 Habanero chiles, roasted, seeded and minced
2 medium cloves of garlic, roasted and minced

2 tbsp. lime juice
¼ tsp. salt

Preparation:

Combine and mash together the chiles and garlic to release the flavors . Serve at room temperature as a really hot picante sauce to add spice to your food. You can dilute the salsa with additional lime juice if you like.

SAUCES

Green Sauce for Papadzules

Ingredients:

10–12 Serrano chiles
2 lbs. tomatillos
1 ½ cups pumpkin seeds
2 cloves garlic, chopped
¼ onion, chopped
1 cup cilantro leaves
2 tbsp. oil
Salt to taste

Preparation:

Boil the chiles uncovered for 10 minutes. Add the husked tomatillos to the pot and cook 5 minutes longer, and drain. In the meantime, toast the pumpkin seeds until they pop.

Pulverize them in a blender or food processor. Add the cooked chiles and tomatillos and the rest of the ingredients and purée until smooth. Makes about 1 quart.

Crema de Ajo—Garlic Cream

Similar to making mayonaise in a blender, this is a tremendous hit with garlic lovers. Use very fresh eggs and take care with the freshness of the garlic. Serve as a spread for crackers or use as a sauce with cooked fish, crab or lobster. Try a little on potato salad.

Grand Daddy crab and lobster with author and husband

Ingredients:
    2 large egg whites, room
        temperature
    3 cloves of garlic, peeled and
        chopped
    ½ medium white onion chopped
    1 tbsp. cilantro leaves
    2 tbsp. lime juice
    1 cup mild flavored extra virgin
        olive oil
    Salt to taste

Preparation:
    Put all the ingredients except the olive oil into a blender and process to a purée. Then add the olive oil in droplets (through the opening in the lid with the blender on medium speed) until the mixture thickens to the consistency of whipped cream. At this point, you can add the remaining oil in a thin stream. When you have added all the oil, taste and add a bit more salt, lime juice and/or cilantro to taste and blend until mixed.
    Variation: substitute chile Xkatic for garlic. Makes 1 ½ cups.

Pipian—Pumpkin Seed Sauce

Ingredients:
    2 dried Guajillo chiles
    2 cups hot water
    1 cup pumpkin seeds
    1 tbsp. vegetable oil
    ½ cup chopped onion
    2 large cloves garlic, chopped
    2 tbsp. recado rojo
    ½ tsp. salt
    ¼ tsp. pepper
    2 tbsp. finely chopped epazote
        (see note below)

Preparation:
    Stem, seed and devein the chiles. Tear them into flat pieces and toast on a medium hot comal or in a heavy skillet, pressing the pieces flat to the hot surface for a few seconds using a metal spatula. Turn the pieces over and press again to toast lightly, taking care not to scorch them. Place in a small bowl, cover with the hot water and let stand for half an hour.
    Toast the pumpkin seeds by putting them in a heated skillet over a medium flame and stirring them constantly until they are popped and golden. (Look out—they can pop hard!)

Remove the seeds to a small bowl to cool and return the skillet to the heat, lowering the flame a bit.

Heat the oil and add the onion and garlic, stirring from time to time, until they are very soft. Now pulverize the pumpkin seeds in a blender. Add the soaked chiles, the onion and garlic mixture, the recado rojo and just enough of the soaking water to make a thick purée. Process for a minute or so, stopping to scrape down the sides of the blender, until the mixture is very smooth. Add the remainder of the chile water and blend well.

Pour the mixture into a heavy 1 ½ quart saucepan, heat it until its hot but not boiling, and continue cooking for 15 minutes, adding the salt, pepper and epazote during the last 5 minutes. Do not let it boil or it will separate. Makes about 3 cups.

Note: If you do not have epazote, use flat leaf parsley, or just forget about it—the sauce will be delicious no matter what!

Cilantro Pesto

Ingredients:
- 2 cups cilantro leaves
- 3 cloves garlic, minced
- ¼ cup pine nuts, toasted
- 1 tbsp. lime juice
- ¼ cup extra virgin olive oil
- Salt and pepper to taste

Preparation:
Put the cilantro leaves, garlic and pine nuts in the bowl of a food processor or a blender. With the motor running, slowly pour in the lime juice and olive oil through the feed tube until the cilantro is puréed. Spoon into a small bowl and add salt and pepper. Makes ½ cup.

Fresh Cilantro leaves

THE JOURNEY

The Caribbean coast of the Yucatán Peninsula has long been a place of pilgrimage. In the days of the ancient empire, Maya women traveled to the island of Cozumel to pray for fertility at the shrine of Ixchel, Goddess of the moon. Guided by beacons set on the high walls of Tulum, seafaring traders brought jade and gold from South America to exchange for salt, cacao, and sea shells. In the sixteenth century, the Spaniards arrived, seeking riches and religious converts.

In the winter of 1983, I arrived in high season to a dark, star-filled night on a two-lane highway shrouded by low jungle on either side. I wanted to become totally immersed in a Spanish-speaking culture in order to learn the language, and I was looking for a place where I could return to "basics." Perhaps most of all, I was looking for my "passion," for something I could really care about doing. As so often happens on journeys, I found even more than I sought.

I first stepped into a Maya kitchen at

Author in search of her passion

a development called Kai Lu'um, an hour from Cancún. Kai Lu'um was famous for its authentic Maya staff and regional dishes, as well as an international menu for hotel guests. Those first steps brought me into a kitchen that was a dim, sandfloored palapa. There I was a stranger to others and to myself. I felt the sideways glances from those dark eyes shining in the giggling smiling faces of my new *compañeras*, women companions.

The kitchen staff consisted of six Maya women. I remember how brightly dressed they were in their colorfully embroidered white *huipiles*, and how they treated me to their handmade corn tortillas. They all competed in a friendly way to make the most perfectly rounded tortilla flexible enough to not crack or break when making a soft taco—a favorite Maya snack. They all moved with such grace that the usual kitchen bumps and spills never happened.

Side by side, we worked without a common language. The sounds of Spanish, English and kitchen Maya blended all day long. How the staff giggled with delight at my desperate attempts to distinguish the subtle tones of the Maya language!

The five teenage waiters (all 14–16 year-old males) were bilingual, with Maya as their first language. Here I was, with 16-plus years of education, and all I had was one language. "*Dios mio.*" "*Que tonta!*" My God, what a dummy! So, my ambition was fired and my kitchen Maya gradually expanded along with my Spanish.

"*Chocc*" was the first Maya word they taught me. "Hot!" A warning word. I stood forewarned. Thank you.

Lupita was the head cook, over five other women and a dishwasher. She and I learned to communicate through intuition and body language along with another worker's translation of my meager Spanish into Maya.

Kai Luum staff photo

In this way, we consulted each other about the daily plan for the kitchen and about what needed to be ordered.

When Lupita lost her job, it was because her husband had made a "drunken *escandalo*," consequently losing his job. Obligated to her husband, she left with him when he returned to their pueblo. It was a sad day for me.

Felipa, who had assisted Lupita, was told to fill her shoes. I mean sandals. Felipa was said to have been one of the most beautiful of Maya women. Her shy courage, sheer faith, acceptance and joy in everything she did were inspiring to me every day.

After eight months of serving up to eighty persons daily, Kai Lu'um closed for its two-month vacation, and I ventured farther in to the Yucatán peninsula.

Arriving in Punta Allen

We were seven adults, eight children. Standing in the back of the black pick-up truck, I was graciously offered a seat on a worn spare tire resting on the bed of the truck. Sensing that the view would be better if I stood, I declined. I was right. But, it was more dangerous too. Ducking overhanging coconut branches with their razor sharp leaves, my eyes scanned right to left, left to right. It was still the rainy season that lasts from May to November, so the road was not dusty. Lush scrub jungle created a living wall to my

Sonja with Caribbean water spout

right. The clear blue sky and the white afternoon sun streaked down from above the green. The road, white sand and *sascab*, a limestone material used in the ancient pyramids, extended through a tunnel of vegetation. Then came the shaky wooden bridge and I could not decide where to look first. My senses were greedy and curious. To the left lay the Caribbean Sea, fed from fresh water canals that still lead back to ancient Maya shrines. White sand extended into a sea at first transparent, then blue, then blue green, and finally the turquoise blue that soothes the mind. Two hours later, we arrived at what was to be my new home.

A short man with strong arms carried two large fish with his hands. He held the tails of the fish off the soft sandy beach by bending his elbows, his forearms braced against his body. Between the fish, just above their heads, was a round, friendly face. After introductions we walked to this fisherman's palapa, a hand-built thatched home.

There he deftly prepared the grouper for the native festival dish Tik in xik. The men tended the pit fire that became the light by which we saw one another. The coconut palms' ruffled leaves made the music until Chaac, a neighbor, arrived with his Sony cassette recorder and a Chico Che tape.

As couples started dancing, I saw the fish again but now it was painted red. The bright red juice of the ancient achiote or annatto tree was blended with selected condiments, making a paste diluted with lime juice. The men had patted this timeless sauce into special diagonal cuts to flavor the flesh of the fish. On top, they spread sliced onion rings and rounds of tomato. They covered the fish with deep green palm leaves and placed it on the embers in the pit. The party peaked when I saw the presentation of the large open fish on a bed of green circular palms. It was served whole for us to feed from, slowly, over a period of time.

Tik In Xik a.k.a. The Painted Fish

The Destination

My quest led me to Punta Allen, where at first, life's necessities dominated my days. Daily priorities included gathering, preparing, and consuming the necessary nutrition. (The gathering consisted of skin diving for spiny lobster, if you want to call that "needed nutrition.") Gradually my language skills improved, but only after my culinary skills.

As I immersed myself in Maya cuisine and hospitality and settled into the rituals of daily life, food and its preparation became the best means of communication with my neighbors. Very few words were necessary (although even these few improved my Spanish). The only essentials were touch, taste, and participation.

The local fishermen cooked deer tail soup, turtle meat, wild boar, *tepesquintle*, and wild turkey, as well as a great variety of seafood. The very best fisherman and cook in my opinion was Armando Lopez, soon to become my partner and husband. When I visited Armando's family in Tizimin, Yucatán, our primary means of communication was again in preparing food.

During my own early cooking experiences in Punta Allen, I cried a lot, shedding many tears because I labored over a smoky open fire, wishing more than anything for a real stove. It came. Then we formalized our kitchen, and instead of eating outside, we ate in our breezy, thatched dining room.

I was constantly surprised at how little I understood techniques, tools, and tastes in my new environment. I felt like a girl again, surrounded by a completely new world of flavors. With English-speaking visitors, I found myself enthusiastically explaining, demonstrating, and serving native dishes—much to their delight. After a time, neither Armando nor I cooked. Instead, we trained native cooks.

I have traveled throughout the Yucatán peninsula with Armando, visiting private homes and various kinds of restaurants. Each year we make a pilgrimage to Armando's hometown in the heart of the Yucatán. There we not only feast on regional specialties with his family, but we also participate in the preparations.

I have been to homes in remote villages hidden in the verdant jungle and facing the open sea. We have found many people skilled in preparing authentic regional meals, most

Ranch kitchen by Pamela Rhodes

of whom consider their ritual-like techniques essential to the nutritional value of the food itself. Some of these recipes date back to the ancient Maya, others are modern, based on new cultivation methods and easily executed in today's kitchen.

Almost no one uses a cookbook here, so recipes and techniques are passed in the oral tradition amidst simmering pots. Most of what is recorded in these recipes has been translated into American equivalents. This is not an effort to include all Yucatecan cuisine, but instead to offer a personal collection gathered during my years with family and friends in the Yucatán Peninsula.

Here in Punta Allen, both new and old cultures determine the way of life. I find my passion at the edge of a clear, constant, yet changing sea, el Mar Caribe, where I have had to learn basic life skills needed in the remote tropics. Here and on roads of the interior, I have been invited to partake of contemporary as well as ancient Maya food. From earthen floored, thatched homes to colonial kitchens of opulent Merida mansions, regional cooking is always presented with pride.

I have personally greeted and hosted thousands of visitors to the Quintana Roo coast of Mexico over the years. In the winter season, English-speaking tourists flock to the Caribbean shores and enjoy the regional food. From now on, I hope they all will return home with a cookbook. Then they can reminisce in the cold, dark days of winter with their own Maya meals.

Hetz'mek

Early on in my new life with Armando, we were asked to be god parents. This is an important relationship, between a godparent and a godchild. Equally important is the relationship between the parents of the child and the godparents. It is so important there is a name for that relationship: *compadres*, or co-parents. When a ritual like baptism, first communion, marriage or school graduation is performed, you no longer call the *compadre* (co-father) or *comadre* (co-mother) by their given names. Rather you use the new title, which is reciprocated: Compadre, Comadre.

The Maya have their own ancient social ceremony, the Hetz'mek, which creates the same type of relationships when a child is still an infant. For a girl, the ritual takes place around three months of age. It has been suggested that the number three correlates to the three hearth stones where women cook. Boys, however, tend to be four months old, which refers to the four directions, north, south, east and west, of the milpa, or subsistence farm, that every Maya man is expected to plant and harvest for the sustenance of his family.

We first performed the Hetz'mek ceremony with Melchor. I straddled him on my hip as was required and then made nine circles around a table whispering to him best wishes for his future. I also handed him a pencil (unsharpened) and a ruler, to wish him scholarly success and a crystal for his health. Then Armando held him astride his hip and circled the table. He had a miniature replica of

Sonja with goddaughter

a lobster gaff (without a barb) to wish Melchor successful lobster fishing in his life. This ritual, older than Christian baptism, provides a social context for creating an extended family. On that day, I accepted the promise to always respect my compadres and to give guidance throughout my life to Melchor. Since then his parents, Arguedo and Chari, have been referred to as compadre and comadre and we have enjoyed participating in Melchor's achievements.

4

AT THE TABLE:
BOTANAS AND APPETIZERS

Botanas are snacks and appetizers that embody the Maya philosophy: take time to enjoy life. Always eaten in a leisurely manner, botanas are offered to guests on arrival, served to workers to lighten the task or savored slowly in the shade during long hot afternoons. They reflect an older lifestyle and bring ritual to a newer one. Botanas are a parade of treats to enjoy with friends.

Travelers in the Yucatán should not miss the chance to try the complimentary botanas that many restaurants feature with every drink order. Some of these restaurants specialize in afternoon entertainments—live shows that range from scantily clad dancing girls to elegant mestizas, women of mixed blood, in traditional dress who drop "bombas" on their audiences. The bombas are jokes. They are Yucatecan Maya humor. Even without understanding Spanish, you can sit back and enjoy the gestures and costumes, the lively music, the superb service, and the taste of each of the plentiful botanas.

Beer is the preferred beverage with botanas, but I usually have wine. Included here is a tequila punch recipe for parties. Many of the following botana recipes can be expanded for luncheon buffet menus, or dinners.

Botanas at the Festival of Tres Reyes

Good eating continues unabated during the final days of the famous Tizimin fair. Though less formal than the chocolomo feast, the preparation and consumption of botanas is no less a ritual. Over the course of a leisurely afternoon, the fortunate guest is treated to a parade of exotic snacks.

Tiny tart plums dipped in ground chile and salt precede *poolcanes*, a Maya word meaning "serpents' heads." These fried cornmeal pastries enclose a filling of white beans and ground pumpkin seeds. To eat, slit open the side of the "serpent's head" and stuff with a spicy salsa of marinated red onion.

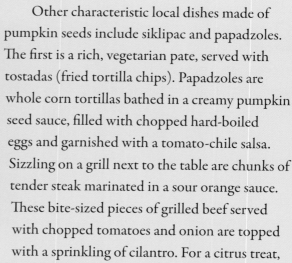

Other characteristic local dishes made of pumpkin seeds include siklipac and papadzoles. The first is a rich, vegetarian pate, served with tostadas (fried tortilla chips). Papadzoles are whole corn tortillas bathed in a creamy pumpkin seed sauce, filled with chopped hard-boiled eggs and garnished with a tomato-chile salsa. Sizzling on a grill next to the table are chunks of tender steak marinated in a sour orange sauce. These bite-sized pieces of grilled beef served with chopped tomatoes and onion are topped with a sprinkling of cilantro. For a citrus treat, savor the freshness of Xeek, a salad of mandarin slices, grapefruit, and crunchy jícama, seasoned with a touch of ground chile.

Meanwhile, laughter, conversation, and ice-cold beer flow with the food. A word of warning for the newcomer: these are snacks, and dinner is yet to come.

The Painted Fish and Other Mayan Feasts

BOTANA RECIPES

Empanadas

Empanadas are a favorite solution for leftovers. Essentially a masa tortilla, an empanada can be stuffed and folded over a myriad of cooked fillings, traditionally a *picadillo* of ground beef or pork, shark in tomato, other fish, or even just beans. Again, a hot salsa serves as a topping.

Ingredients:
> 1 ½ cups masa harina
> 2 tbsp. white flour
> ¾ cup warm water
> ¾ cup filling (see above)
> Oil
> Onion and Habanero Salsa
>   (see page 32)

Preparation:
> Mix the masa harina to soft dough, using a bit more water if needed. Divide the dough into 12 equal parts and roll into balls. Cover with a damp cloth to keep from drying out while you complete the recipe. Make tortillas, either by hand or by using a tortilla press, 3 ½ to 4 inches wide. Leaving the uncooked tortillas on the plastic sheet, put a scant tablespoon of the filling on one side of the uncooked tortilla—not too close to the edge. Put the palm of your hand underneath the plastic and fold the other half of the dough over the filling and press the edges together gently to seal. Heat oil (a depth of ½ inch) in a large frying pan. Fry for about 2 minutes on each side until golden brown. Drain on paper toweling. Serve hot with Onion Salsa. Makes 12.

Deluxe Ceviche

Ceviche is the standard lunch where I live. It is marinated raw fish, or shellfish, or both. One reason for the distinctive taste is that the lobster, conch, fish, octopus, shrimp and/or crab combinations are fresh, caught daily. There are variations to ceviche from region to region. This recipe is from the state of Quintana Roo.

Ingredients:
> 2 cups raw lobster, conch, scallops, firm
>   white fish, or any combination,
>   cut into small pieces
> ½ cup lime juice
> ¼ cup chopped red onion
> ¼ cup chopped seeded tomatoes
> 2 tbsp. chopped cilantro
> Minced seeded Habanero to taste
>   (start with ½)

Salt and pepper to taste
1 tbsp. extra virgin olive oil

Preparation:

Mix the seafood and the lime juice. Let stand for 20 minutes. Stir in the rest of the ingredients except the olive oil. Cover loosely and let stand another 10 minutes or so, until the fish is translucent. Just before serving, stir in the olive oil. Serves 4 to 6.

Ceviche demonstration at Sian Ka'an Artists

Green Mango with Chile Piquin

Sour tastes accentuated by hot chile seem to be a favorite on places south of the tropic of Cancer.

Ingredients:

2 mangoes, fairly ripe, but still green
Juice of 1 lime
½ tsp. each powdered chile Piquin and
    salt, mixed together

Preparation:

Place each mango stem side down on a cutting surface, narrow side toward you. Cut through vertically on both sides of the seed. Lay each half flat and, with a small sharp knife, cut a cross hatch, being careful to leave the skin intact. Hold the sides firm with your thumbs while pressing upward with your fingers on the center portion of the peel to form a convex (see illustration). Sprinkle with lime juice and the chile Piquin-salt mixture.

Note: This can also be prepared with bite-sized pieces of peeled mango and served as a side dish. Serves 4.

Guacamole with mucho cilantro

Guacamole

Very popular now with many variations, this is our favorite recipe. Leaving the pit in the final product ensures its bright color for many hours. Serve with tostadas. Great for crowds.

Ingredients:
    2 large ripe avocados
    Juice of 1 lime
    1 small white onion, finely chopped
    1 tomato, seeded and finely chopped
    ¼ cup chopped cilantro
    Salt to taste
    1 Habanero chile, seeded and minced
    3 tbsp. lime juice
    Pinch of salt

Preparation:
    Peel the avocados and mash the pulp. Mix in a bowl with the lime juice, chopped onion, tomato, cilantro and salt. In a small bowl, mix the minced Habanero and lime juice. Serve on the side add according to individual tolerance. Serves 4.

Avocado and Salsa Appetizer

For sit-down dinners, serve this attractive presentation instead of guacamole, though it requires the same ingredients.

Ingredients:
    2 avocados, fully ripe but not too soft
        (Hass are best)
    ¼ cup Xnipek, more or less

Preparation:
    Cut each avocado lengthwise through to the pit and twist to separate the halves. Holding the half containing the pit in the palm of your hand, carefully give the pit a hit with the blade of a chef's knife and turn to remove, leaving a tidy cavity. Cut a small slice from the peel side to flatten for stability, and place each half on a plate and spoon Xnipek into the cavities. Serves 4.

Demystifying jícama

Xeek Mixed Citrus and Jícama Salad

Xeek translates from Maya as "mixture." For a citrus treat, savor the freshness of Xeek, a salad of mandarin slices, grapefruit, and crunchy jícama, seasoned with a touch of ground chile. To refresh the palate, serve this traditional New Year's salad cold. It is crunchy and juicy and demystifies jícama, its major ingredient.

Ingredients:

1 cup orange segments
1 cup grapefruit segments
1 cup tangerine or mandarin orange
    segments
½ cup jícama, peeled, sliced crosswise
    thinly, slices cut into sticks
    about ½ by 1 inch
¼ cup lime juice
Pinch of powdered chile Piquin or
    Cayenne pepper

Preparation:

Using a small, very sharp knife, remove seeds, white part and membrane from fruit segments. Halve the orange segments, cut the grapefruit into thirds and leave the tangerine sections whole. Combine the fruit with the other ingredients in a serving bowl, mixing well. Serve chilled or at room temperature. Serves 4 to 6.

Salbutes

Lijia, a passionate cook and dear friend, started a *lonchería*, a small restaurant, serving *salbutes*, *panuchos*, *tortas* or sandwiches and chicken soup every evening. These are typical fare for supper as the main meal served in the afternoon before *siesta*. At Lijia's first restaurant, she used shredded chicken in almost all of her dishes. Hours before opening, while passing by enroute to the town square

Cooking demonstration at Living Adventure workshop

Ingredients:

1 ¼ cups masa harina
¾ cup warm water
Vegetable oil for frying
1 ½ cups shredded chicken or pork
1 ½ cups cabbage salsa
Salsa Xnipec and/or any other salsas

Preparation:

Mix the masa harina and the water to make soft dough, following the directions for tortillas on page 12. Divide the dough into 12 pieces and flatten each piece into a 2-inch round. Make tortillas about 4 inches in diameter.

Heat 1 or 2 heavy griddles or skillets until a drop of water sizzles. Lightly oil the surface and cook the tortillas, turning the first time when the edges just begin to dry. Let the second side cook until a few brown spots begin to show, then turn back again to the first side until the center is puffed, pressing the center with a wadded paper towel to encourage the puffing. As they are cooked, stack them and keep them warm wrapped in a cloth napkin.

Pour cooking oil into a skillet to a depth of ¼ inch and heat. Cook the tortillas, without crowding in the pan, just until they hold their shape but are not yet crisp. Drain on paper

two blocks away, I would see her and her staff calmly, carefully shredding mounds of cooked and cooled chicken for her restaurant. Later, when I would arrive to buy food *"para llevar"* or "to go," they would still be patiently shredding the chicken as she had a brisk business and would need all that was prepared. One night there was a lull in the stream of customers and I asked Lijia if she could show me how to make these tasty treats. Her good nature and cooking expertise have provided me with many a dish. This was the first one she demonstrated and I still remember that hot kitchen and her encouraging words as I fumbled along making my first salbutes.

A simple variation of its cousin the panucho, the salbute is good at suppertime or as a breakfast treat. Use shredded leftover meat, like roast chicken, turkey or pork.

toweling and arrange on a heated platter. Top with shredded chicken or pork (or both) and cabbage salsa. Serve with Xnipec.

Note: Additional toppings might include diced avocado, olive wedges, toasted pumpkin seeds, crumbled cheese and chopped pickled Jalapeños. You can set out small dishes of a variety of these and let guests have at it as they like. Serves 4 to 6.

Panuchos

Evening meals are what we might call supper. Although time consuming to make, the local panucho/salbute stand provides these tasty treats for snacks or appetizers or simply supper.

Ingredients:
> 1 ½ cups masa harina
> ¾ cup water
> 1 ½ cups frijoles colados (see page 130)
> Oil for frying
> 1 ½ cups shredded chicken, well
>   seasoned with salt
> 1 ½ cups cabbage salsa (see page 32)
> 2 plum tomatoes, halved, seeded
>   and cut into thin lengthwise
>   strips
> 1 recipe Salsa Habanero (see page 31)

Preparation:

Mix the masa harina and the water to make soft dough. Cover with plastic and let stand for half an hour. Divide the dough into 12 pieces and flatten each piece into a 2-inch round. Make tortillas, either using a tortilla press or by hand according to the directions on page 12, 3 ½ to 4 inches in diameter.

Heat 1 or 2 heavy griddles or frying pans until a drop of water sizzles. Lightly oil the surface (a wadded paper towel works well for this) and cook the tortillas, turning the first time when the edges just begin to dry. Let the second side cook until a few brown spots begin to show, then turn back again to the first side until the center is puffed. Pressing gently with the wadded paper towel encourages this action. As they are cooked, stack them and keep them warm in a heavy cloth.

Take the tortillas out, one at a time, and make a small slit around the edge, lifting up the thin layer of dough that puffed up when the tortilla was cooking, stuff the pocket with a large spoonful of the frijoles colados and press the dough back down over the slit. In a skillet, heat oil to a depth of ¼ inch and fry the panuchos until crisp.

Put on a heated platter, top with cabbage salsa, shredded chicken and tomato slices.

Serve with Salsa Habanero. Serves 4 to 6.

Yucatan cattle at Rancho San Victor

Kibis de Res—Beef Kibis

I was shocked the first time my sister-in-law served these flavorful botanas to me and then I understood that it was an influence of the Lebanese community.

Ingredients:

½ cup bulgur
1 cup boiling water
2 tbsp. oil
1 lb. ground beef
½ cup finely chopped bell pepper
1 large clove garlic, minced
½ cup finely chopped white onion
Salt and freshly ground black pepper to taste
1 tbsp. fresh mint, finely chopped, or 1 tsp. dried
Additional oil for frying

Preparation:

Put the bulgur into a heatproof container and pour the boiling water over it. Stir,

Traditional Kibis

mint. Mix well. Form into patties about ½ inch thick and 3 inches in diameter (about ¼ cup for each patty), and place on a cookie sheet lined with parchment or waxed paper. Fill a large skillet to ¼ inch deep with oil and heat to medium hot. Drop the patties into the oil (do not crowd them) and fry, turning once, until browned on both sides. Drain on paper toweling. Keep the *kibis* hot in a 200-degree oven until all are cooked. Serve on a heated platter with cabbage or salsa. Makes 12 kibis.

Kibis de Venado o Borrego— Venison or Lamb Kibis

Prepare as for Kibis de Res using ground or finely chopped venison or lamb instead of beef.

Kibis de Caracol

The only kibis I knew before living on the peninsula was made of ground beef. Apparently, the Lebanese community brought this recipe here as well. Then, my sister-in-law, Chari, surprised me by making kibis from ground conch meat. She is an expert at frying these tasty patties to perfection and serves them topped with the customary cabbage salsa.

cover, and let stand for half an hour. In the meantime, heat the 2 tbsp. oil in a medium sized skillet and sauté the onion in the oil for about 5 minutes. Add the bell pepper and garlic to the onion and cook over low heat, stirring from time to time, until the vegetables are tender. Add to the soaked bulgur (water should be entirely absorbed—if not, let it stand a bit longer), together with the ground beef, salt and pepper and chopped

Ingredients:

½ cup fine bulgur
1 cup boiling water
2 tbsp. vegetable oil
½ cup finely chopped white onion
3 cloves garlic, minced
½ cup finely diced green pepper
2 tbsp. lime juice
2 tbsp. chopped fresh spearmint
2 tbsp. chopped parsley
½ tsp. salt, or to taste
Salt and pepper to taste
1 lb. ground conch (see note)
½ cup fine, dry bread crumbs
Vegetable oil for frying

Preparation:

Combine the bulgur with the boiling water, cover and let stand for half an hour. Meanwhile, heat the 2 tablespoons of oil in a skillet. Add the onion, garlic and green pepper and sauté until tender. Remove from the heat and add the lime juice, chopped mint and parsley. Add the mixture to the soaked bulgur together with the ground conch, and the bread crumbs. Mix well and season with plenty of salt and pepper. Form into patties about ½ inch thick and 3 inches in diameter (about ¼ cup for each patty), and place on a cookie sheet lined with parchment or waxed paper. Fill a skillet to ¼ inch deep with oil and heat to medium hot (360 to 375 degrees). Drop the patties into the oil and fry (do not crowd them), turning once, until browned on both sides. Drain on paper toweling. Keep the kibis hot in a 200-degree oven until all are cooked. Serve with Cabbage Salsa (see page 32). Makes about 12.

Note: For the ground conch, put the meat through a food grinder using a ¼-inch plate, or else cut into ½-inch cubes and pulse in a food processor until finely chopped.

Queen Anne Conch

Lobster Salpicón

Ingredients:

2 cups chopped cooked lobster
¼ cup finely chopped onions
¼ cup chopped tomatoes
¼ cup finely chopped radish
¼ cup sour orange or lime juice
2 tbsp. chopped cilantro
Minced Habanero chile to taste
    (start with ½)
Salt and pepper to taste

Preparation:

Combine all the ingredients in a medium sized bowl and serve at room temperature with crackers or tostadas. Serves 4 to 6.

Polcanes—Serpents' Heads

These fried masa pastries enclose a filling of white beans and ground pumpkin seeds. To eat, slit open the side of the "serpent's head" and stuff with a spicy salsa of marinated red onion.

Lobster catch by Armando

The Painted Fish and Other Mayan Feasts

Ingredients:

    2 cups masa harina
    1 ¼ cups water
    1 tsp. salt
    ½ cup toasted ground pumpkin seeds
    1 cup cooked white beans, including
        about ¼ cup bean broth
    ¼ cup minced red onion
    1 recipe Salsa Habanero (see page 31)

Preparation:

Mix the masa, water, chile and salt to make dough. Combine the pumpkin seeds with the beans. Divide the dough into 12 pieces and form into balls. Flatten between sheets of waxed paper or plastic into rounds about 4 inches in diameter and no more than ¼ inch thick. Remove the top sheet of paper and put a heaping tablespoon of the bean mixture into the center of the masa. Close the masa around the filling to form an oval, tapering at the ends. Pinch the ends tightly closed to form your "Serpent's Head" and place on a paper or foil lined sheet pan. Cover with a damp cloth. Repeat until all the polcanes are formed. Pour oil to a depth of about ½ inch in a large skillet. Heat to medium hot and fry the polcanes a few at a time until golden brown on both sides. Do not crowd the pan or the polcanes will not be crisp.

Serve hot with minced red onion and Habanero salsa. Makes 12.

Sikli' P'aak—Toasted Pumpkin Seed Dip

This Maya botana is a very light creamy vegetarian blend, which I call Maya paté. It is served with tortilla chips or, non-traditionally, with fresh vegetable sticks. Generally, it is made very picante or hot. Suit yourself.

Ingredients:

    1 lb. tomatoes (3–4), flame roasted,
        seeded, peeled and chopped
    ½ Habanero chile, or more, roasted,
        seeded, peeled, and minced
    ½ cup toasted, ground, pumpkin seeds
    2 tbsp. cilantro, chopped fine
    Salt to taste

Preparation:

Combine the ingredients in a small bowl and serve slightly chilled or at room temperature. Serve as a dip with tostadas. Makes about 1 cup.

Note: ground roasted pumpkin seeds can be found in shops specializing in Mexican and Central American products. Toasting and grinding your own are preferable.

5

THE LAND OF THE PHEASANT AND THE DEER

Fowl

Deep in the forest dwell the *zip* (spirit winds in deer form). Deer pull the sun across the sky on short days; peccaries, much slower animals, pull it on long ones, according to Maya belief. Turkeys sacrificed to the gods are featured frequently in classic Maya art. The Maya have always used native game as a source of protein, but wisdom and reverence surround these foods.

New Year's Day 1988

Tipi *número uno* (our first thatched tipi). Pinta, my kitty, is at my feet on a new serape. Her brother, Negro, is circling the screen enclosing the bottom of the thatched tipi. Last night's New Year's Eve party was the first one I ever hosted. The menu was planned days in advance, and everyone helped with the slaughter of a turkey that Mimi, a long-time friend and fellow foodie, and I bought for forty pesos.

Walking vendors often come through Punta Allen. This week,

two young boys carried six live turkeys, their feet tied and threaded onto a strong pole. When Mimi and I wanted to look at the turkeys, the boys handed us a skinny one, but we knew better. After checking each of the larger looking birds by feeling their thighs and breasts through their feathers, we choose the meatiest one.

We tethered the turkey in the yard and fed it popcorn kernels. Luckily Pasqual, our bird dog, made peace with *el pavo* (the turkey). The men's job was to prepare the turkey with chicken and pigeon in the Pibil style—a Maya meal cooked in a pit of hot coals covered over with sand to seal in the heat. The meat stays moist as it cooks in a blend of its own juices and "Maya barbecue sauce," achiote or recado rojo.

Mimi and I saw the preparations when we went to Lupe's house. In his back yard, we all raised a little brandy in a toast to the old year and the new. The botanas, or appetizers, included fresh coconut, toasted chambray onions, green mangoes with chile and salt, refried beans, guacamole, and tortilla chips.

The men had already slaughtered the turkey and plucked its feathers. Mimi and I sat down and chatted with Victor, our Mayor, while we watched Lupe and Mustafa prepare the meat, vegetables and achiote sauce. They thinned the achiote with lime juice, spread it over the meat, and rubbed the sauce into the skin. They lined a large caldron with the center veins of banana leaves to insulate the food from the hot coals of the pit. The meat went into the pot, along with generous rounds of tomatoes, onions and potatoes.

In the meantime, the men dug a pit in the sand near the three new thatched tipis on our corner lot. They arranged the firewood carefully so it would burn and drop further down into the pit to make coals for the Pibil. The covered pot went into the pit, covered with sand, and left for one hour. Then we removed it, separated the potatoes, tore the meat into pieces, combined it with the onion and tomatoes, and placed it in warm tortillas to make tacos. The juice from the pot was served on the side, along with the potatoes and black beans.

Braised Duck Cuzan

Raisins, olives and capers provide a Middle Eastern slant to a universal bird.

Ingredients:
>1 duck (5–6 lbs., including giblets)
>4 large cloves garlic
>1 large white onion
>6 Roma tomatoes
>1 bay leaf
>1 tbsp. oregano
>½ cup orange juice
>½ cup dry sherry
>1 cup duck stock (see recipe directions)
>Salt and pepper
>3 tbsp. raisins
>3 tbsp. Spanish style green olives, pitted
>   and cut into wedges
>1 tbsp. capers

Preparation:

Rinse the bird well and pat dry with toweling. With a small sharp knife cut down on both sides of the backbone in order to remove it. Take off the skin, chop the backbone into several pieces and put in a 1 ½ quart sauce pan together with the giblets, a pint of water, 1 ½ teaspoons salt and 4 whole peppercorns. Bring to a boil and let simmer for half an hour to make the stock. In the meantime, roast the tomatoes, quartered onion and garlic in a medium hot comal or under a broiler. Let them cool enough to handle, then coarsely purée in a food processor or a blender and set aside. Now cut the duck into 6 pieces. Trim excess skin and remove fat. Prick the skin in several places on each piece being careful not to pierce the flesh. Sauté the duck in a hot, dry frying pan until well browned. Pour off all but 1 tablespoon of the accumulated fat. Add the tomato purée to the pan together with the orange juice, sherry and duck stock (be sure to skim off any fat). Stir the mixture carefully, scraping up the brown bits at the bottom of the pan. Bring to a boil, lower the heat, cover and simmer for 45 minutes. Add raisins, olives and capers and cook an additional half an hour. Transfer the duck to a heated platter. Skim off any floating fat from the sauce, boil it down a bit if it seems too thin, taste for salt and pepper, pour it over the duck and serve. Serves 2 to 3.

Chicken Campeche

For several years, Ester, along with her husband and two daughters, lived in the downstairs apartment from us in Felipe Carrillo Puerto, where we had our office and part time residence. This was a good thing. She always toasted and ground all of the ingredients for this classic chicken delight and was always ready to show me techniques and to share the prepared food with me.

Nacho consulted with Donna a lot over this recipe, from the most western state on the peninsula. It makes a nice change for Sunday afternoon chicken dinner.

Ingredients:

1 chicken (3 to 3 ½ pounds), rinsed and dried and cut into 8 pieces
¼ cup lime juice
Salt and freshly ground black pepper
3 tbsp. olive oil
1 large onion, chopped
3 large cloves garlic, minced
1 large green pepper, chopped
4 plum tomatoes, seeded and chopped
1 Xcatik, Anaheim, or yellow hot pepper, roasted, peeled, seeded, deveined and chopped finely
½ tsp. thyme
½ tsp. marjoram
½ tsp. salt
½ cup dry sherry
½ cup chicken broth
¼ cup prunes, pitted and cut into slivers
¼ cup Spanish style green olives, pitted and cut into wedges
¼ cup almonds, blanched, chopped and toasted
1 tbsp. chopped parsley

Preparation:

Sprinkle the chicken with the lime juice, salt and pepper and let stand, turning a few times, for half an hour. Heat 2 tbsp. of the olive oil in a skillet and sauté the chicken in batches until golden brown and remove to a stovetop casserole. Add the remaining 1 tbsp. olive oil to the skillet and cook the onion, garlic and green pepper over a medium flame until soft. Add the tomatoes, chile, thyme, marjoram, and salt, and cook about 5 minutes longer. Add the sherry to the pan and let it come to a boil, stirring and scraping the bottom of the pan. Add the chicken broth, prunes and green olives; bring to a boil and spoon over the chicken pieces in the casserole. Cover, bring to a boil, lower the heat and let it simmer for about 20 minutes. Transfer the chicken to a heated platter and top with the toasted almonds and chopped parsley. Serves 4.

Ester's Pollo Escabeche con Buut—Pickled Chicken with Pork Rolls

Escabeche in this area refers to a combination of spices including cloves, allspice and oregano. Serve in shallow bowls with plenty of broth, chicken and the *buut*.

Ingredients:

 1 cut up frying chicken, about 3 lbs.
 Salt and pepper
 1 tbsp. vegetable oil
 3 cups chicken broth
 1 recipe recado for escabeche (see page 28)
 1 bay leaf
 Buut (see recipe below)
 2 heads garlic
 2 Habanero chiles
 1 chile Xcatik, or any other pale yellow chile
 1 tbsp. vegetable oil
 3 tbsp. white wine vinegar
 2 medium red onions halved lengthwise and sliced into ¼-inch crescents
 Additional salt and pepper to taste

Preparation:

 Heat 1 tbsp. oil in a heavy Dutch oven and sauté the chicken until golden, turning once. Add the water and bring to a boil, skimming off any foam that accumulates on the surface.

Lower the flame, stir in the recado and add the bay leaf. Carefully lower the buut into the pot, cover and cook for half an hour. Flame roast the garlic and chiles until about half the skin is charred. Rub off the blackened bits and add to the pot. Cook an additional 10 minutes, turn off the heat and set aside.

Transfer the chiles, garlic and 1 cup of the chicken broth to a 2-quart saucepan. Add 1 tbsp. oil, the vinegar, onions, salt and pepper (be generous with the pepper), and cook for 10 minutes.

Take the chicken out of the pot. Skin and bone the pieces and tear the meat into chunks. Place in a heated serving dish, together with the buut. Separate the garlic into individual cloves and add to the dish. Ladle the onions and broth over the chicken and serve. Serves 4.

Buut—Pork Meat Balls

Buut can be either extra large meatballs or several smaller ones with a cooked egg yolk in the center, served with relleno negro and escabeche. Each dish has different ingredients in its meatballs. This one is for escabeche. Buut is sometimes wrapped in cheese cloth or gently placed in the simmering "mother pot" and cooked thoroughly. I always make sure my plate has a generous serving of buut.

Buut with egg

Ingredients:

    1 lb. lean, finely ground pork (have a lean
        piece of loin ground to order)
    8 green olives, pitted and chopped fine
    1 tbsp. raisins, chopped fine
    1 tbsp. capers
    2 Roma tomatoes, seeded, cored and
        chopped fine
    ¼ cup minced green pepper
    ¼ cup minced white onion
    2 raw eggs
    Salt and freshly ground pepper
    4 hard boiled eggs, the whites minced,
        the yolks left whole

Preparation:

Mix well all the ingredients except the hard-boiled yolks. Divide the mixture and

form into a firm ball around each yolk and gently place in the simmering escabeche

Pollo a la Orange—Chicken in Orange Sauce

When I first saw this on a menu, I thought the French must have brought it, though now I see it as an invention from available ingredients.

Ingredients:

    4 small chicken breasts or large halves
    2 tbsp. lime juice
    Salt and pepper to taste
    1 large Guajillo chile pepper, stemmed,
        seeded, deveined and toasted
    ½ cup very hot water
    2 tbsp. vegetable oil
    2 large cloves garlic, minced
    1 cup tomato purée (make your own or
        use canned)
    1 cup freshly squeezed orange juice
    1 tsp. orange zest
    1 tsp. oregano
    1 stick Mexican cinnamon
    1 tbsp. chopped chives

Preparation:

Rub the chicken breast with lime juice and

sprinkle with salt and pepper. Put the Guajillo chile to soak in hot water. Let stand for half an hour while you assemble the remaining ingredients. Heat the oil in a frying pan and sauté the chicken breasts, skin side first, until they are just golden. Transfer to a heavy casserole dish, cover to keep warm. Lower the heat under the frying pan and add the minced garlic. Cook for a couple of minutes without browning. Add ½ cup of the orange juice to the pan to deglaze it, scraping the brown bits up from the bottom. Purée the chile and water in a blender and mix in a small pot with the tomato purée, cinnamon stick, oregano, orange zest and the rest of the orange juice. Bring to a boil and let simmer uncovered for 10 minutes. Strain the sauce through a medium mesh onto the chicken, bring to a boil, cover the pot and let simmer for 20 minutes. Arrange the chicken breasts on a heated platter and spoon on the sauce, which should be just thick enough to cover the chicken. Boil down or thin with additional orange juice as necessary. Sprinkle with chopped chives. Serves 4.

Chicken with Beer

This is an adaptation by Donna that includes popular ingredients like chile, oregano, and pumpkin seeds.

Proud Rooster at Rancho El Angel

Ingredients:

1 chicken (3 to 3 ½ pounds), rinsed and
    dried
3 tbsp. vegetable oil
½ cup flour
1 tsp. salt
½ tsp. pepper
¼ tsp. powdered Habanero or Cayenne
    pepper
½ cup beer
½ cup tomato purée
1 cup rich chicken stock (see below)

1 Xcatik, Anaheim, or yellow Italian chile
　　pepper, roasted, peeled, seeded,
　　deveined and cut into strips
4 large cloves garlic, roasted, peeled and
　　halved
1 tbsp. toasted, crumbled oregano
2 tbsp. lime juice
2 tbsp. finely chopped toasted pumpkin
　　seeds
2 tbsp. chopped cilantro

Preparation:

Using a small, sharp knife, remove the
neck, back, wings and feet (if it still has them)
from the chicken and reserve for stock. Cut
the breast into 4 pieces and separate the legs
from the thighs. Heat the oil in a large frying
pan. Mix the flour, salt, pepper, and chili
powder. Dredge the chicken pieces in the
seasoned flour and sauté in the hot oil until
golden brown. Remove from the pan, and
keep warm. Deglaze the pan with the beer.
Add tomato purée, chicken stock, chile strips,
garlic cloves, and oregano. Bring to a boil,
reduce heat to a simmer, cover and cook for
half an hour. Remove the chicken to a heated
platter. Add the pumpkin seeds and lime juice
to the sauce. Add additional salt and pepper if
necessary. Pour the sauce over the chicken and
top with cilantro. Serves 4.

Fajitas, Maya Style

Since Mexican food popularity made Fajitas
a household word, we started cooking the
chicken with achiote to give this a Maya bent.

Ingredients:

4 boned chicken breasts (1 ½–2 lbs.)
　　cut in lengthwise strips ½ to ¾
　　inches wide
¼ cup orange juice
2 tbsp. lime juice
1 tbsp. recado rojo
⅓ cup olive oil
4 cloves of garlic, peeled and crushed
　　with the flat of a knife blade
½ tsp. salt
Freshly ground pepper to taste
2 large green bell peppers, seeds and
　　membranes removed, cut into ½
　　inch strips
2 large onions, halved lengthwise and
　　cut into ½ inch crescents
Additional oil for frying

Preparation:

Put the chicken breasts in a glass or
ceramic container. Mix the juice, recado rojo,
orange and lime juices, olive oil, garlic, salt
and pepper and pour over the chicken. Turn
a few times to coat well. Cover loosely and

let marinate, turning from time to time, for 2 hours. Heat oil to medium heat at a depth of ¼ inch in a large frying pan. Add the bell peppers and onions and cook quickly just until tender. Remove from the pan and set aside. Add a bit more oil to the pan, heat it up, and add the chicken strips. Cook over high heat, stirring often, until they are cooked through and lightly browned. Return the bell peppers and onions to the pan, heat, stir for a few moments, and turn the mixture onto a heated platter. Serve with warm flour tortillas and any or all of the following: Xnipec or other salsa, guacamole, diced tomato, finely chopped red onion, frijoles refritos, chopped cilantro. Serves 4 to 6.

Grilled Chicken and Achiote

This basic chicken recipe is fine on its own, but is also used in other dishes like salbutes and panuchos or tacos.

Ingredients:

    3 lb. broiling chicken, cut in half, or use
        halved chicken breasts (4 small
        or 2 large, halved
    2 tbsp. achiote paste
    2 tbsp. sour orange or lime juice
    2 tbsp. olive oil

Preparation:

Smear the outside of the chicken with a mixture of achiote paste and sour orange and let stand for half an hour. Brush with olive oil and grill or broil until the juices run clear. You can also sauté the chicken. Serve as is for a main course or cool, shred, and use for salbutes, panuchos or tacos.

Dzik Shredding Technique:

Chicken is shredded for salbutes, panuchos, chicken salad or tacos. You will be amazed at the volume of meat you can produce from only one chicken by taking the time to carefully shred it. After cooking and cooling a chicken, use both hands to tear smaller and smaller shreds from each piece of meat that you take off the bones. This is the same as the *dzik* technique used with red meats.

Boiled Chicken

A universal preparation of chicken, the broth of boiled chicken can be used to make chicken soup, nature's cold remedy, even in the Yucatán. If the chicken is needed for a salad or tacos, remove, cool and then shred as described above.

Ingredients:

1 whole chicken, approximately 3 lbs.
Garlic
Oregano
Salt and pepper

Preparation:

Quarter the chicken and place in a saucepan with other ingredients and cover with water bring to a boil, cover lower heat and cook until done.

Pollo Pibil

Clearly the most traditional of chicken dishes, Pollo Pibil is found on most menus throughout the Yucatán. Be sure to try it if traveling on the peninsula. Otherwise, improvise in the following manner:

Ingredients:

1 chicken (about 3 lbs.) quartered, or 4 small chicken breasts
1 ½ tbsp. recado rojo paste
½ cup sour orange juice, or a mixture of half orange and half lime juice
2 cloves garlic, peeled and mashed
3 banana leaves, the fibers from the spines removed and pulled into long threads

3 plum tomatoes cut lengthwise into eighths
1 medium white onion, halved lengthwise and cut into thin strips
4 tsp. best quality olive oil
4 sprigs fresh epazote (optional)

Preparation:

Combine the recado rojo paste with the juice. Pour over the chicken pieces and turn to coat. Marinate half an hour, turning once.

To assemble the Pibil, form a mat of banana leaves for each packet. Make it at least 2 layers thick and approximately 12 by 18 inches, leaving a cross of fibers under the leaves. Place a chicken quarter in the center of each banana leaf mat, then divide the tomato wedges and onion slices between them and sprinkle with the olive oil. Fold the long ends of the banana leaves over the center of the chicken, then the short ends, under the first, as you would a gift package. Tie and knot securely with the fibers from the banana leaves. Repeat for each package.

Use a steamer pot fitted with a rack or steamer basket. Fill with water up to the bottom of the basket. Place the Pibil in the basket. Bring the water to a boil, lower the heat, and steam until the chicken is tender, about 1 hour.

In the meantime, combine the ingredients for the salsa and set aside.

When done, remove the chicken and serve each packet individually. Pass the salsa. Serves 4.

Onion Salsa

Ingredients:

 1 medium red onion, minced
 ⅓ cup sour orange juice, or a mixture of
  half orange and half lime juice
 Pinch of salt

Preparation:

 Mix ingredients and serve.

Quail Sian Kaán

Though hunting is restricted in the Biosphere reserve, quail has become very accessible in American markets. Try this for a special dinner.

Ingredients:

 8 quail, 6–8 oz. each
 2 dried Guajillo chiles
 ¾ cup very hot water
 ¼ cup dry sherry
 ¼ cup honey
 1 cup strained, freshly squeezed orange
  juice
 4 cloves garlic, minced
 1 tsp. salt
 ½ tsp. coarsely ground black pepper
 1 tsp. oregano
 4 tbsp. vegetable oil
 1 tbsp. chopped chives

Preparation:

 Stem, seed and devein the chiles. Tear them into flat pieces and toast them on a medium hot comal or in a heavy skillet, pressing them flat to the hot surface for half a minute. Flip the pieces over and press again to toast lightly. Don't char them or they'll be bitter. Put the chile pieces in a small bowl and pour the hot water over them. Let stand for half an hour.

 In the meantime, cut the birds through the backbone with poultry shears or a small sharp knife. Open them up and place them on a flat surface, skin side up. Press down on the breastbone firmly with the heel of your hand, cracking the bones slightly until the birds lie flat. Rinse and dry them and place in a single layer in one or more glass or non-reactive metal pans.

 Pureé the chiles with their water in a blender. Add the sherry, honey, orange juice, garlic, salt, pepper, oregano and process a few moments to blend. Pour the marinade over the quail. Cover loosely and let marinate, refrigerated, for at least 2 and up to 6 hours, turning from time to time.

Heat the oil in a heavy ovenproof skillet over medium high heat. Remove the quail from the marinade and brown on all sides being sure not to crowd them in the pan (you'll need to do this in batches, keeping the browned birds warm while you do the others).

Put all the quail back in the pan, breast side down, and place in a preheated 375-degree oven. Roast for 5 minutes, basting with the marinade and the juices that accumulate in the bottom of the pan. Turn them over and roast another five minutes, basting again. Arrange them on a heated platter, pour the juices over and sprinkle with chopped chives. Encourage diners to eat with their fingers. Serves 4.

Roast Pheasant with Sweet Potatoes

Since the peninsula has long been dubbed "The Land of the Pheasant and the Deer," I was eager to learn a delicious pheasant dish. What I learned instead: what is translated as pheasant is actually curassow, a large black bird with a distinctive top knot, which can be seen on the back roads of the Sian Kaán Reserve as well as the road to our ranch. The curassow's population has decreased markedly since colonial days but there are now concerted efforts to protect this stately bird.

This recipe uses the common pheasant found in the U.S. and Donna developed it especially for me.

This outstanding dinner for two should be for a special occasion with candlelight. The glaze gives the pheasant a gorgeous color on the outside while leaving succulent white meat inside.

Ingredients:

1 pheasant, 2–3 lbs.
Salt and pepper
1 clove garlic, crushed with the flat of a knife
½ tsp. oregano
1 small white onion, sliced
¼ lime
2 tbsp. vegetable oil
2 tbsp. honey
2 tbsp. orange juice
2 tbsp. Sherry wine vinegar
2 coarsely chopped canned chipotle peppers in adobo

2 medium sweet potatoes, cooked until
barely tender
1 tbsp. chopped chives
Mango salsa or Salsa Chiltomate

Preparation:

Preheat oven to 375 degrees. Sprinkle the
pheasant inside and out with salt and pepper.
Place the garlic clove, sliced onion, lime wedge
and oregano in the cavity. Tie the legs together
with string and tuck the wings under.

Place the oil, honey, orange juice, vinegar,
and chipotles in a blender and process a
minute or so until puréed. Brush some of
the glaze over the bird and put it, breast side
up, on a rack in a baking pan. Roast, basting
frequently, until tender and the juices run pale
pink—45 to 50 minutes.

Peel and slice the potatoes into ½-inch
thick rounds. When the bird is cooked,
remove it from the pan onto a platter and set it
aside. Heat a skillet and add to it a tablespoon
or two of the accumulated dripping from the
pan. Sauté the potato slices until they start
to brown a bit, brushing with some of the
remaining glaze. When cooked, arrange the
potatoes around the pheasant and sprinkle
with chopped chives. Serve with tropical salsa.
Serves 2.

Relleno Negro de Pavo—Turkey with Spiced Chile Paste

This dish is traditionally made with turkey,
but certainly a chicken or two would suffice.
I do warn you of a dark flavor and sinister
sight most unusual to the eye, so try it first
on trusted family and friends or any itinerant
warlocks who might happen by.

Ingredients:

1 small turkey, about 8 lbs., cut into
serving pieces
2 heads garlic, flame roasted
10 tbsp. recado negro (see page 27)
1 white onion, minced
4 plum tomatoes, minced
1 sprig epazote

Preparation:

Bring a pot of water to a boil, season
with salt and add the turkey. Flame roast the
garlic and add to the pot. Prepare and dilute
the relleno negro spice paste in a little of the
cooking water, then strain the concoction into
the pot with the turkey.

Add onion, tomatoes and epazote.

In the meantime prepare the buut (recipe
below) and carefully lower the balls of pork
into the cooking pot.

Buut for Relleno Negro

Ingredients:

    2 lbs. ground leg of pork
    1 tsp. epazote, minced
    2 plum tomatoes, minced
    2 raw eggs
    1 tsp. salt
    1 tsp. black pepper
    4 hard-boiled eggs, whites minced,
        yolks separated

Preparation:

    Mix all the ingredients well except the yolks. Form equal-sized balls of the mixture around the yolks. Gently add the meatballs to the relleno negro.

Huevos Divorciados—Divorced Eggs

EGGS AND CHEESE

Huevos Divorciados—Divorced Eggs

I had a good laugh when I first saw these fried eggs topped with contrasting salsas of red and green. To insure the divorced style of these eggs, serve refried black beans in between the fried eggs topped with the complimentary colored salsas.

Ingredients:

    8 fried eggs, sunnyside up
    1 cup green salsa
    1 cup red salsa
    Refried beans, optional

Preparation:

    Serve two eggs per person, topping one with red salsa, the other with green. Serves 4.

Huevos con Chaya—Eggs with Chaya

I introduce this dish as food of the ancient Maya gods. You can substitute spinach for the chaya.

Ingredients:

    8 large eggs
    ½ tsp. salt
    2 tbsp. water
    2 tbsp. olive oil
    4 tbsp. finely chopped white onion
    1 large clove garlic, minced
    2 cups chaya leaves, or small spinach,
        coarsely chopped
    1 cup Salsa Xnipec
    ¼ cup crumbled queso fresco
    1 minced Habanero chile
    ¼ cup lime juice

Preparation:

Put the lime juice in a small condiment bowl, add the minced chiles and set aside. Whisk together the eggs, salt and water. Heat the oil in a large skillet (non-stick works best) over a medium flame. Add the onion, garlic, and fry until soft, but not browned. Stir in the chopped chaya or spinach and sauté until wilted. Add the egg mixture to the skillet and cook, turning the mixture with a heavy plastic or wooden spatula until the eggs are set and almost, but not quite, dry. Spoon onto a heated platter. Serve with Salsa Fresca, queso fresco and the chile in lime juice. Serves 4.

Torta de Yerba Buena—Egg Omelet with Spearmint

I like to quiz our guests to test their taste buds when serving this unusual combination of spearmint with eggs.

Ingredients:

    8 large eggs
    2 tbsp. mint, cut crosswise into thin
        ribbons
    2 tbsp. butter
    Salsa Chiltomate

Preparation:

Make four flat omelets using two eggs whisked together with a tbsp. of mint for each. Melt half a tablespoon of butter in a hot, 8-inch non-stick skillet. Pour in the egg mixture and fry until firm but not dry. Turn out onto a heated plate. Serve with Salsa Chiltomate. Serves 4.

Hardboiled Eggs with Chiltomate

This is a favorite way to have hard-boiled eggs, warm or at room temperature, smothered with Chiltomate salsa with a hot corn tortilla.

Ingredients:
　4–8 eggs
　Chiltomate Salsa
　Hot corn tortillas

Preparation:
　Put the eggs in a pot just large enough to hold them. Add cold water to cover by ½ inch.
　Bring the water to a full boil, cover the pan, and let stand off the heat for 20 minutes.
　Drain and run cold water over the eggs until you can handle them and then peel them. Halve the eggs and serve with Chiltomate Salsa and hot corn tortillas. Serves 4.

Huevos a la Mexicana—Eggs Mexican style

Especially easy to make (after all the chopping of ingredients) as it is simply a Mexican salsa in scrambled eggs.

Ingredients:
　2 tbsp. oil
　¼ cup onion, finely chopped
　4 Roma tomatoes, cored, seeded
　　　　and diced
　8 eggs, lightly beaten
　Salt and pepper to taste
　Simple salsa Habanero

Morning ritual in outdoor kitchen

Preparation:
　Heat the oil over medium high heat and sauté the onions until they turn a light brown. Add the tomatoes and cook for about 2 minutes, or until softened. Add the beaten eggs and cook, stirring, until done to your liking. Serve with Habanero salsa and warm corn or flour tortillas. Serves 4.

Huevos Motuleños

Named for the town of Motul in the state of Yucatán, this recipe adds chopped ham and canned peas (often used in Latin America) to fried eggs on corn tortillas that are smothered in refried beans.

Ingredients:

4 tomatoes, peeled, seeds removed and
   chopped
1 medium onion, chopped
2 cloves garlic, chopped
1 tsp. oregano
½ tsp. salt
1 chile Xcatik or yellow hot wax chile,
   whole
2 tbsp. oil
Oil for frying
4 corn tortillas
Oil for frying
4 eggs
1 cup heated frijoles refritos
½ cup cooked peas
½ cup chopped cooked ham
½ cup crumbled white cheese
Fried banana

Preparation:

Put the tomatoes, onion, garlic and
oregano into a blender and purée until
smooth. Heat 2 tbsp. oil in a pan and cook
the purée together with the whole chile over
a high flame for a few minutes, stirring often.
Remove from the heat and keep hot. Heat ¼
inch oil in a skillet. Fry the tortillas to soften,
making sure they don't become crisp, and
drain on paper toweling. In the same pan,

cook the eggs just until they are set.

To put together, place 1 tortilla on a
heated plate and spread with the beans. Place
an egg on the prepared tortilla, pour the sauce
(take out the whole chile) over the egg and
top with peas, ham and cheese. Fried slices of
plantain bananas or platano de comida always
accompany this dish. Serves 4.

Papadzules—Egg Enchiladas

Papadzules are whole corn tortillas bathed
in a creamy pumpkin seed sauce, filled with
chopped hard-boiled eggs, rolled up and
garnished with a tomato chile salsa. Serve any
hour of the day.

Ingredients:

6 large eggs, hardboiled and chopped fine
Salt to taste
12 corn tortillas
3 Guajillo or Ancho chiles, toasted,
   seeded and deveined
½ white onion, chopped
1 large clove garlic, chopped
1 cup tomato purée
1 cup water
1 tsp. salt
2 tbsp. oil
Additional oil for frying

Green Pipian sauce (page 34)
¾ cup crumbled queso fresco (optional)
see following note

Preparation:

Put the chiles in a small bowl, cover with hot water and set aside for half an hour. Drain them and put in a blender together with the onion, garlic, tomato purée, water and salt. Purée until smooth. Heat the oil in a medium sized skillet, then add the sauce and simmer for about 5 minutes, stirring often. Keep warm.

Pour oil to a depth of ¼ inch in a frying pan and fry the tortillas lightly on each side. Drain briefly on paper toweling and stack them to keep them warm. Ladle a little of the sauce into a heated 9 by 12 serving dish. Working quickly, dip each of the tortillas into the sauce, fill with some of the chopped egg, roll up and arrange side by side in the dish. Top with any additional sauce and ladle the Pipian Sauce down the center. Serves 4 to 6.

Queso fresco—Fresh cheese

Often crumbled on top of botanas, *queso fresco* is made from milk that is clabbered and dried into curds. It has a slight acidity, can be creamy or very dry, and adds contrasting color when sprinkled on top of red or green salsas.

Green Pipian sauce

DAVID MILLER AND ECO-TOURISM

Earthwatch Team

October 22, 1994, Rollo May died this week. His obituary said that he was a humanist, or one who tried to relieve human suffering without delving into the past. That reminded me of a late gray afternoon when Armando and I were sitting at our outdoor eating table. We were in the middle of lobster head soup when Armando looked up toward the path leading to his property. I followed his gaze and saw a tall blond man taking large strides toward us. The man walked with a gentle relaxed rhythm, without much movement of his arms.

"Who's that?" I asked, amazed at the myriad of visitors who found their way to this little corner of the earth.

"Doctor Miller," said Armando as he stood up to greet him with the hug, back slap, and handshake customary between men.

Doctor Miller introduced himself as David. It was clear from his manner that he had been here before. I went to the open fire and spooned out some of the lobster head soup for him, and Armando found him an ice-cold beer. We talked for hours. David asked about the other fishermen of the town and their families. David had been studying the local lobster fishery over a period of years and had returned to update his data. As he rose to leave that evening, David said he could tell that I was very fond of Armando.

"I am too," he said. "I believe Armando is the only true humanist that I know."

The following year when David returned, he found us re-located to a beach house a block away. Here we all followed his custom of drinking a cold beer and eating his favorite dish, *caracol en mojo de ajo*, de Armando, conch in garlic cooked by Armando.

This time, David wanted us to consider hosting "Earthwatch" groups to further his lobster fishery studies. We had begun to accommodate tourists, but they were rare. At that time, the area was not yet a biosphere reserve and the road was inviting only to the intrepid. Still, we had begun. We agreed between ourselves that Earthwatch would be a viable first project.

The next day, Armando and I were in his launch preparing to go fishing. David was hitching a ride on a visiting sailboat to Playa del Carmen before returning to upstate New York. As our vessels passed and we shouted good byes, we then confirmed our business deal verbally though we were mere ships passing. David Miller's faith in our ability paved the way for our venture into the ecotourism industry.

Alux, The Leprechaun of the Maya

Maya legends tell of people who are no more than two feet tall, but very strong. They are said to imitate all types of animals and birds and sometimes persons and things. Although you can hear them talk, you'll never see the *Alux*. Sometimes they can frighten you. Alternatively, the Alux may make mischief—like rearranging your tools so that you can find yourself searching for something you were certain you left in a particular corner or place. They also help guard the milpa during the night, so food is left out for them on all four corners of the site.

I've taken to blaming the Alux when I can't find my glasses. Maybe they have something to do with unmatched socks.

Ruin site on Punta Allen Road

Bateya

During my early days in Punta Allen, I was the scandal of the homemakers in my barrio or neighborhood. They thought that I might not be getting my clothes clean due to my method of hand washing in a bucket. Of course, everyone else also washed by hand—no electricity, no washing machines. However, according to tradition, one should have a proper washtub, a *bateya*.

Armando threatened to get one, but I stubbornly used my two five-gallon white buckets filled with detergent and water. I either hauled water from our well or pumped it with a salvaged bilge pump adapted to our shallow well. Then, as the business was developing, I realized that if I ever wanted help with the laundry I would have to conform.

Finally, our first bateya arrived. It was very "typical," as it was made of wood (unlike the currently popular cast-composite bateya). When the wooden bateya wears out, it is recycled as the kind of backdoor raised-bed garden so often seen here.

To recycle the shallow laundry sink into a raised planter, the container is elevated on four long legs to chest height. This makes it easy to sow and harvest. It also inhibits backyard animals from destroying or eating the plants. The converted bateya would typically hold any or all of the following: cilantro, chive, epazote, leaf lettuce, radishes and chile Habanero.

Brooms

I've noticed that many people here tend to use a regular stand-up household broom with a push technique, rather than a sweeping motion that I am used to. It always reminds me of my first broom in Punta Allen. It was a handsome, handmade, natural palm leaf broom with a straight jungle pole handle and vine string fastening. This attractive, rustic coastal tool is definitely not designed for "sweeping." The push method of brooming used in today's modern Maya home seems to be a vestige of the palm leaf broom.

6

HARVEST FROM THE SEA

Gratitude

From the Gulf Coast to the Caribbean, contemporary Maya delight in delicacies from the sea as did their ancestors. On one of our 90-mile drives to Felipe Carrillo Puerto, I had a chance to learn first-hand the kind of gratitude still practiced by the modern Maya. Though Armando is from a mestizo family, he feels his Maya heritage very strongly. He frequently says, "*Soy Maya*" (I am Maya).

Although we left early at five a.m. to avoid the heat, we had several errands along the way. The night before, Armando had prepared the Gott ice chest with the last of the ice. (Ice comes twice weekly from Tulum on a route truck.) We didn't want to leave the place iceless, but the day before I had caught a large barracuda and Armando had shot some snapper with his speargun. We needed the ice to make the trip with our catch that we planned to give some friends in an inland town.

We were driving our yellow, carpeted van. Our last hour on the road was around noon. There we were, traveling from early morning into the noonday sun, with only a small, barely-sufficient piece of ice over the fish. The rest was water, though fortunately still below the level of the drain hole, which had lost its stopper.

81

When he suddenly spotted one of the Yucatán's famous giant speed bumps or *topes*, Armando made an abrupt stop. (By the way, they call the topes "dead policeman" in Costa Rica). As the van slid over the tope, water sloshed in the cooler, splashing up and out through the drain hole and spurting in waves onto the carpet. It left an aroma. That is the word I have learned to use about this smell when I am trying to be magnanimous.

Anyway, I found it profoundly unpleasant, and I fretted about the work it would take to shampoo the carpet to eradicate the odor. After the third bump, I was really feeling jostled, and wondered when Armando would stop more gently. At every shift of the gears, another puff of aroma of fishy water filled the enclosed van—even though I had my window open.

I can't remember what I said, but Armando stopped the van and turned to me. He raised his open palm, lifting it and lowering it in emphasis of his words: "*Soy pescador.*" I am a fisherman. (Doesn't it appear wonderful, marvelous, that here we are: me a fisherman and I have fish for my friends?)

The Painted Fish and Other Mayan Feasts

Crocodiles

Ascension Bay was once known for its crocodiles. According to my biologist friends, there are two kinds of crocodiles in this area. One species, Morelet's crocodile *Crocodylus moreleti*, which has a broad, flat snout, prefers the swamps, rivers and ponds of the interior. The American crocodile *C. acutus* has a long, narrow head with big eyes and teeth, and ranges all along the coast from fresh water to brackish saltwater.

My compadre used to be one of the most successful crocodile hunters, going on all-night forages into the mangrove lagoons around the bay. After the prohibition of their slaughter for food and skins, my compadre took to lobster fishing. He says the pay is not as good, but the hours are better.

Sian Ka'an crocodile

Manatee

The manatee is now protected in the biosphere. Once slaughtered for oil and for meat that is said to compare with pork, manatee families are still seen around "*ojos de agua*," or natural freshwater springs in the bay and lagoons. While looking for washed-up bamboo we found a manatee carcass on a deserted beach. It apparently had beached and died. I had some of the bone worked and discovered its value as a carving medium. We keep some bones on hand for others to see.

Don Jose and Salted Fish

I'll never forget the hot summer day that I climbed the ladder/stairway to the sleeping room in our pyramid-shaped palapa, stepped into the darkness, and was overwhelmed by a strong odor. I stopped, closed my eyes, took a deep breath through my nose and released it, rapidly.

"Ugh," I said to Armando, stretched out on his stomach in his blue and white hammock.

"*'Ta bien*," (it's good) he said in reply.

"*No, no ésta bien*," I said emphatically.

Armando flipped over. With cocked head and outreached arm, he indicated a place behind and above my left shoulder. There, draped over a stick supported by the thatched wall and wooden ladder to the lookout, was a 20 pound barracuda. This barracuda dangling there in my bedroom had been carefully cleaned and dressed. Salt was rubbed into each slice, and only the skin held the entire fish together.

Open-mouthed, I watched as fish oil dripped onto my rough cut ironwood (Chechen) floor. I turned and saw Armando's smiling face propped into his hand, his elbow stretching the threads of his hammock. I know my face crinkled into annoyance.

"Doesn't that smell bad to you?" I asked in Spanish.

"Bad? Bad? I am salting and drying that fish to give to Don José. It will be from us."

Then I thought of Don José, and how much he loved the abundance of salted fish he had eaten in his youth. Today, with the availability of ice and propane refrigeration, salt is seldom used as a means of preserving fish.

From deep within me came a sigh of surrender as I claimed my resting space in Armando's hammock and nodded, "*Está bien*."

Salting Whole Fish

First remove scales and then splay open a whole fish. Remove the central spinal bone leaving the two sides intact with the support of the skin. Score the flesh every inch and a half to the skin. Use kosher or sea salt and rub it into the flesh of the fish and into all the crevices and slits. Hang to dry in a place safe from cats!

Costa Maya dried fish

Sea Turtles

Sea turtles, now an endangered species throughout the world, are protected and often seen in the waters of Quintana Roo when you spend enough time at the right spots. Only recently accustomed to spending an entire day out fishing in an open boat, I spotted a large, yard-long turtle shell above the waterline. Armando turned the boat in the direction indicated, and we realized there were two turtles mating.

Continuing to stare I reached into my bag and grabbed my camera. I had to look down to detach the leather cover, remove the lens cap, raise the camera to my eye, and adjust the setting. Half of my brain was taking the picture while the other half was trying to observe the turtles. I snapped the shot, and the turtles dove beneath the water together just as I lowered the camera.

Sonja preserving turtle eggs

Wedding at Holbox

Gretchen is a friend from the States who is studying the Maya language. Early one morning, she and I took our usual walk on the beach. We strolled across countless seashells embedded in the white sand, still damp from the receding tide of the Gulf of Mexico. When we returned, we found Armando ready to leave on a launch. He was eager to swim, fish, and catch some lobster.

Our guide, Milano, agreed to harvest a few conch for a ceviche as his pay. Our friend Baron and his compadre, a visitor from Tabasco, went along too. Gretchen and I sat in the launch with them and soaked up the warm sun on our shoulders.

Armando hung onto a rope line behind the boat, and we towed him to each lobster habitat. Armando himself gaffed three lobsters. After four years of retirement from the lobster cooperative in Punta Allen, he hadn't lost his touch.

Later, the men prepared a spectacular ceviche to share at the wedding of Martin and Siena. Don Manuel and Doña Margarita, the bride's parents, served lobster salad, ceviche, turkey relleno, and champagne to 400 or more guests.

The newly married couple stood behind eight single layers of wedding cake displayed in the shape of a heart and posed for pictures with honored guests. All eight cakes were served.

A five piece band provided the rhythm for "*coliando*" or "tailing." The bride and groom stood on chairs in the middle of the large dance floor, and the groom held the train of his bride's wedding gown high. First, the single women danced in a line under the train and around in front of the bride. As they did, she poured champagne into their mouths and later over their heads.

The tension mounted. Finally, the bride threw her bouquet of white flowers to the eager participants and someone happily caught it.

Next, the more plentiful married women formed a conga line, one behind another.

Wedding in Holbox

Holding each other's waists with both hands and dancing vigorously, they passed beneath the train, around the groom, and under the train again. They finally passed in front of the bride. She poured more champagne into the waiting (and some not-too-eager-to-drink) mouths. These women commented that if they had a chance to catch the bouquet, perhaps they would soon marry for a second time.

By then, the blazing afternoon sun shone into the courtyard dance floor. Everyone took a short rest from the heat, but then the groom stepped up on his chair again. From the surrounding shaded tables of guests, the bachelors headed for the dance floor.

Tailing with bride and groom

Soon another conga line was swaying, singing, and swallowing their share of *caña*, or sugarcane liquor, which the groom poured into their waiting mouths.

Suddenly, the bachelors grabbed the groom and pulled him down from his perch on the chair. One friend sat on his stomach to hold him. Then the young men lifted the groom and threw him into the air—one, two, three times. Next, the bachelors tried, one by one, to remove some of the groom's clothes. They succeeded in taking off his white jacket, then black boots and red bow tie. Dancing, singing and shouting all the while, they carried him to a nearby room. The door to the room opened and they all crowded in. Then the door closed.

Shortly afterward, the door opened and the single men filed out of the room each dancing and flinging about a piece of the groom's wedding outfit. They surrounded the bride and she danced inside their circle, her veil now covered with paper pesos collected earlier from the guests.

Finally, the young men, teasing the bride with her new husband's garments, guided her to the room where they had left her husband—surely without any clothes on. The bachelors gently pushed the bride inside the dark room, throwing her husband's clothes in behind her. Immediately three small children hurried to the doorstep and peeked under the door. Amid laughter and applause, they hastily retreated and waited with the rest of us for the couple to emerge.

When they did, the groom, showered and dressed though still missing his jacket carried his bride to the wedding table.

Fishing Tournament, Mahajual, 1996

Today, Armando is separating the head of a sailfish from the skeleton of its body. He will give the head to a young boy who wants to preserve it and add it to his collection of other species of fish. The 59-pound vela was caught by Filipe Delgado's crew on the Maja: Victor, Shel, and Chino. They will receive a plaque for the largest fish in the tournament.

They also placed second after Armando Ferret of Cancún for another category, measured in points per species times its weight in kilos. Cuzan brought in dorado, or dolphin fish, each day—four the second day. One weighed 45 pounds.

Armando's catch

The day before the tournament, Armando and his crew—Abel, known as *el Tigre*, and our dear friend Pepe Salazar—traveled by launch from Punta Allen. I came from Carrillo Puerto by way of Chetumal, bringing appropriate food and equipment to camp on the beach. Fortunately, the Delgados have a lovely new beach house and we were able to share their hospitality, including that of their daughters, Maja and Rebecca and their dog, Bones.

There were heavy gusting winds and rain the night before the tournament. I didn't go out on the boat the first day because storms were still passing through. In spite of my boating experience, I remain a fair-weather sailor. Of course, as soon as the others left, the skies cleared and the wind calmed.

I was left on shore to visit with my hostess and enjoy the festivities of the *torneo*, backgammon and dominoes competitions and a children's fishing tournament. At the only restaurant in town we enjoyed fresh fried hogfish and snapper topped with marinated red onions. In the evening we danced on the beach to 'Bubbles,' a traveling disco troupe which featured both live and canned music. The M.C. was very animated and verbose, which encouraged us to get up and participate. We enjoyed the natural-sand dance floor as we danced the Macarena.

Teal and Lily, champion fisherwomen

FISH AND SEAFOOD

Lobster Fishing in Punta Allen (Javier Rojo Gomez)

The town of Punta Allen is known for its well-organized lobster fishing cooperative. Here, equipped with snorkel, mask, fins and a gaff, local fishermen catch the common spiny lobster (Panulirus Argus) from artificial habitats or *casitas*. These "little houses" are flat surfaces about a meter square made by the fishermen and placed on the sea floor in their campo or designated fishing area. From July first to March first, members of the cooperative bring in over thirty tons of lobster tails to be sold internationally.

Spiny lobsters are very gregarious and like to hang out together in dark places. Not very particular about food, they eat small, shelled creatures, worms and other weaker animals. From March to July, the enlightened Mexican fishing industry prohibits lobster harvest as they are mating and spawning. During mating, the male lobster produces a sticky fluid containing sperm that he deposits on the underside of the female. The surface of the fluid quickly hardens forming tar spots

frequently seen on female lobsters. A short time after mating, the female lays bright orange eggs that attach beneath her tail. To fertilize the eggs she scratches the surface of the tar spot to release the sperm contained inside.

An adult female spiny lobster can lay about 500,000 eggs at one time. The eggs hatch in about four weeks. The larvae, defenseless, float on the water, carried many miles by currents and are eaten by fish and other marine animals. In their next stage of life, they are called pueruli and have the shape of a lobster but their shells are colorless and soft. Now they settle in shallow coastal areas including reefs, seagrass beds and mangroves. Ascension Bay, to the south of Punta Allen is a natural nursery for the spiny lobster. As the lobsters grow, they molt, losing their hard shell and growing a new larger covering. They later move into deeper waters, growing approximately one inch a year. Adult lobsters measure three to three and a half inches of carapace length. Lobsters with backs shorter than three inches have not had a chance to reproduce and are left in the sea until they reach adult size.

Management of lobster fisheries is increasingly strict, requiring new markets and new techniques such as capturing live lobsters with nets thrown around the artificial habitats.

This enables fishermen to throw back females with eggs and immature lobsters. Additionally, there is less waste as the full live body is sold as opposed to only the tails.

The Punta Allen Lobster Cooperative is well known and respected nationwide for its stringent regulations, which helps ensure the fishermen and their families will prosper for years to come.

Breaded Lobster

A Cuzan House specialty. The trick here is to butterfly the tail before breading. This is absolutely one of the richest, most delicious ways to eat lobster.

Ingredients:
    4 spiny lobster tails
    4 tbsp. lime juice
    4 large cloves garlic, minced
    ½ tsp. each salt and pepper, or to taste
    1 cup fine dry breadcrumbs
    2 tbsp. flour
    2 well beaten eggs
    Vegetable oil
    4 lime wedges

Preparation:
    Cut away the soft undercover of the tails with a pair of scissors. Then, take a small sharp knife and slit through the center of the back of the shell starting from the tail and guiding the knife with your index finger. Remove the meat from the shell leaving the fan of the tail attached. Cut ¾ of the way through the meat and flatten with the palm of your hand to butterfly. Sprinkle with lime juice, salt and pepper, and spread with the minced garlic. Let stand for half an hour.

Mix the breadcrumbs and flour in a shallow plate. Using the tail fan as a handle, dip the lobster first in the beaten egg and then in the breadcrumb and flour mixture. Make sure the crumbs cover the entire surface of the meat. Place on a rack to dry for about 20 minutes at room temperature (if you chill the breading it will absorb too much oil when cooked).

Heat the oil in a large frying pan to a depth of ¼ inch and fry the lobster for about 5 minutes on each side until golden brown. Drain on toweling and arrange on a heated platter. Garnish with lime wedges. Serves 4.

Lobster Mojo de Ajo

This is possibly the most popular way to get one's garlic fix. *Mojo* is a marinade principally of *ajo*.

Ingredients:

4 spiny lobster tails in the shell, cut
open
4 garlic cloves, minced
2 tbsp. each lemon and lime juice
4 tbsp. oil
Lime wedges

Preparation:

Mix the garlic, lemon and lime juices and
spoon onto the lobster meat. Let stand for ½
to 1 hour. Heat the oil in a large frying pan.
Place the lobsters in the pan, meat side down.
Cover and cook for 4 or 5 minutes until lightly
browned. Turn, lower the heat and cook,
covered, another 5 minutes. Put on a heated
platter and garnish with the lime wedges.
Serves 4.

Nacho's Lobster Filled Potato Cakes

One year in Punta Allen there was a town
cooking contest for lobster. I received second
place with this recipe my dear friend, Nacho,
the fabulous cook, taught me. I presented
them on fresh banana leaves for color
contrast.

Ingredients:

2 ½ lbs. potatoes, peeled and quartered
1 tbsp. melted butter
¼ cup milk
1 tsp. salt
1 tsp. black pepper
1 tbsp. vegetable oil
¼ cup white onion, minced
2 cloves garlic, minced
1 ½ cups cooked lobster meat, finely
shredded
1 cup flour
1 tsp. salt
½ tsp. pepper
2 eggs beaten with 1 tbsp. water
Fine dry breadcrumbs
Additional vegetable oil for frying

Preparation:

Boil the potatoes in salted water until
tender. Drain and mash. Add the melted
butter, milk, salt and pepper. Beat to a purée
with a heavy wooden spoon and set aside. Heat
the tablespoon of oil in a frying pan. Add the
onion and sauté until transparent. Add the
garlic and cook a couple of minutes longer.
Add the shredded lobster and cook, stirring,
another minute or so until heated through. Set
aside to cool.

Shape the potato mixture into 16 balls. Place each ball in the palm of your hand, flatten it and press a rounded tablespoonful of the lobster mixture into the center. Form into cakes less than an inch thick. When all the cakes are made, dip them first in the flour, then in the beaten egg seasoned with salt and pepper, and lastly in the breadcrumbs. Place on a sheet of waxed paper or plastic wrap. Fill a frying pan to ½ inch deep with vegetable oil and heat to medium hot. Fry the cakes until golden brown on both sides in batches, turning once. Remove cakes with a slotted spoon to drain on paper toweling. Add more oil to the pan as necessary, letting it heat up before continuing frying. These will serve 8 as an appetizer, 4 as an entrée.

Serve with Xnipek. This is an excellent first course followed by grilled fish, black beans and cabbage ensalada.

Lobster with pasta

Pasta with Lobster Sauce

In the old days, fresh vegetables and fruits, even tomatoes were not always available in Punta Allen. So, when Donna, a visiting chef, came up with this recipe it was a great help to me as the shopper.

Ingredients:

2 spiny lobster tails, about 1 ¼ lbs. each
4 tbsp. recado rojo
4 cloves garlic, minced
¼ cup bitter orange juice, or a mix of
    equal parts orange juice and
    white wine vinegar
¼ cup vegetable oil
2 large white onions, chopped
4 large cloves garlic, pan roasted, peeled
    and halved

2 chiles Xcatik, roasted, peeled, seeded
    and chopped
1 tbsp. toasted oregano
2 cups seafood stock or chicken broth
Salt and black pepper to taste.
4 tbsp. epazote, coarsely chopped (if
    epazote isn't available, use
    parsley or chives)
1 lb. linguine, cooked, drained and
    tossed with a tbsp. of olive oil

Preparation:

Mix the recado rojo and the minced garlic.
Dilute to a thin sauce with the orange juice.
Spread over the lobsters, reserving any extra.
Let stand for at least an hour. Heat the oil in a
sauté pan until medium hot. Place the lobsters
in the pan, meat side down. Cover and cook
until lightly browned. Turn them and continue
to cook until done. Remove and set aside.

Strain the oil and wipe out the pan. Return
the oil to the pan and sauté the onions in it
until golden. Add the roasted garlic, chiles
Xcatik, oregano, stock, reserved juices, and
boil for 5 minutes. Taste the sauce and add salt,
pepper, and additional recado mixture if you
want to intensify the flavor.

Meanwhile, remove the lobster meat from
the shells, reserving any juices. Cut the meat
into bite-sized pieces and set aside. Bring the
sauce to a simmer, add the lobster meat and
heat through. There should be plenty of liquid
for dunking garlic bread. Place the linguine
in individual bowls, top with the sauce, and
garnish with chopped epazote. Serves 4 as a
main course or 6 as a first course.

Langosta con Leche de Coco—Lobster with Coconut Milk

This is a fine combination as both major
ingredients complement one another.

Ingredients:

2 tbsp. vegetable oil
1 medium onion, diced
4 plum tomatoes, seeded and diced
1 chile Xcatik, seeded and thinly sliced
4 cloves garlic, crushed with the flat of a
    knife blade
1 tsp. dried oregano
½ tsp. salt
1 tsp. black pepper
4 spiny lobster tails, in the shell
½ tsp. salt
½ tsp. black pepper
1 ½ tbsp. recado rojo, dissolved in
    ½ cup water
2 cups coconut milk (see note below)

Preparation:

Heat the oil in a frying pan. Sauté the onion until translucent, about 5 minutes. Add the tomatoes, chile Xcatik, garlic, oregano, salt and pepper and cook the mixture, stirring from time to time, for about 15 minutes or until the vegetables are cooked and the juices have evaporated. Put the lobster tails in a pot just large enough to hold them in one layer.

Add the recado dissolved in water and just enough additional water to cover. Bring to a boil over medium heat. Add the coconut milk and the sautéed vegetables. Lower the heat, cover, and bring to a boil again. Remove from the heat and serve in deep bowls. Serves 4.

Note: Ripe coconuts contain a mild liquid, which should be discarded. To prepare coconut milk from a ripe coconut, pare the brown skin from the coconut meat. Chop the meat and blend with 2 cups scalded water. Let stand for 20 minutes and strain (2 cups packaged dried unsweetened coconut can be substituted for fresh).

Lobster Pizza

Ingredients:

½ recipe pizza dough (see below)
Cornmeal
2 tbsp. olive oil

4 tbsp. freshly grated parmesan cheese
½ cup cilantro pesto (see page 36)
Meat from a spiny lobster tail, shelled as described in the Breaded Lobster recipe, and shredded . About ¾ lb.
1 tbsp. oregano
Salt and pepper to taste
4 oz. mozzarella cheese, grated
4 tomatoes, roasted, peeled, seeded and diced
2 chiles Xcatik, roasted, peeled, seeded and cut into thin strips

Preparation:

Preheat the oven to 500 degrees. Lightly oil a pizza pan and sprinkle lightly with cornmeal. On a well-floured board, press out or roll the pizza dough into a circle about 12 inches in diameter and lift the dough onto the prepared pizza pan. Brush the entire surface with olive oil, then pinch edges to make a border about ½ inch high. Sprinkle the parmesan and spread the cilantro pesto evenly over the dough. Mix the lobster, oregano, salt, pepper, and place on top of the pesto. Arrange the diced tomatoes and chili strips decoratively on top and bake 15 to 20 minutes until the crust is nicely browned. Serves 4.

Pizza Dough
Ingredients:

    1 cup warm water
    1 pkg. active dry yeast or ¼ oz.
        compressed yeast
    2 ½ to 3 cups unbleached all-purpose
        flour
    2 tbsp. olive oil
    ½ tsp. salt

Preparation:

Mix the water, yeast and 1 ½ cups of the flour in a large bowl. Mix well. Add the oil, salt, and remaining flour. With your hands or a heavy wooden spoon, work the ingredients together until the dough holds its shape (you may need a bit less flour, so add the last half gradually).

Place the dough on a lightly floured surface and knead until it is smooth and elastic, about 5 minutes. If the dough becomes sticky while you are kneading it, sprinkle a bit more flour over it.

Transfer the dough to a lightly oiled 2-quart bowl. Turn so that the top of the dough is oiled, cover with a towel, and let rise until doubled—about an hour. When the dough has risen, divide it in half and shape into balls. Cover with a towel and let rest for 15 minutes. The dough is now ready to shape, top and bake.

Spiny lobster feast

Lobster with Recado and Garlic

Ingredients:

    4 spiny lobster tails, about 1 ¼ lbs. each
    2 tbsp. recado rojo
    4 garlic cloves, minced
    2 tbsp. each lemon and lime juice
    4 tbsp. vegetable oil
    Lime wedges

Preparation:

Mix the recado rojo, garlic and lime juice and spread over the lobster meat. Let stand for an hour. Heat the oil in a large frying pan until medium hot. Place the lobsters in the pan, meat side down. Cover and cook for 4 or 5 minutes until lightly browned. Turn, lower the heat and cook, covered, another 5 minutes. Put on a heated platter and garnish with the lime wedges. Serves 4.

Ensalada de Langosta—Lobster Salad

Lobster salad is another of my favorites. This is a basic potato salad that can be converted into lobster or chicken salad. It is very typical throughout the peninsula and requires shredding or tearing the meat.

Ingredients:

1 ½ cups shredded, cooked lobster*
2 ½ cups cooked, cubed potatoes
½ cup chopped onions
1 ½ cups cooked, cubed carrots
3 hard-boiled eggs, chopped
1 cup mayonnaise
1 small can green peas, drained
Salt and pepper to taste

Preparation:

In a large bowl, place the lobster, potatoes, onions, carrots, eggs, mayonnaise and peas. Stir gently to combine. Add salt and pepper to taste. Chill. Serves 4.

*You can make this recipe with shredded chicken instead of lobster. Add the juice of canned Jalapeños to taste.

Crab filled Potato Cakes

Very delicate flavor with the comfort of potato makes this process worthwhile.

Ingredients:

2 ½ lbs. potatoes, peeled and quartered
¼ cup milk
1 tbsp. melted butter
1 tsp. salt
½ tsp. black pepper
1 tbsp. oil
¼ cup white onion, minced
¼ cup green onion, minced
2 cloves garlic, minced
4 Roma tomatoes, peeled, seeded and finely diced
1 ½ cups crab meat, shredded
1 cup flour
1 tsp. oregano
1 tsp. salt

½ tsp. pepper
2 eggs beaten with 1 tbsp. water
Fine dry breadcrumbs
Oil for frying

Preparation:

Boil the potatoes in salted water until tender. Drain and mash. Add the melted butter, milk, salt and pepper. Beat to a purée with a heavy wooden spoon and set aside. Heat the 1 tbsp. oil in a frying pan and cook the onion, green pepper and garlic until tender. Add the tomato and cook 5 minutes longer.

Mix in the crabmeat, add salt, and pepper to taste. Combine the flour, oregano, salt and pepper and turn out onto a plate or a pie pan.

Shape the potato mixture into 16 balls. Place each ball in the palm of your hand. Flatten it and press a rounded tablespoon of the crab mixture into the center. Form into cakes less than an inch thick. When all the cakes are made, dip them first in the seasoned flour, then in the beaten egg, and lastly in the breadcrumbs. Place on a sheet of waxed paper or plastic wrap.

Fill a large frying pan to ½ inch deep with oil and heat to medium hot. Fry the cakes until golden brown on both sides in batches, turning once. Remove the cakes with a slotted spoon to drain on paper toweling. Add more oil to the pan as necessary, letting it heat up before continuing frying. Serve with Xnipek. Serves 8 as an appetizer or 4 as a main dish.

Pounding conch and octopus

Breaking down muscular fibers by pounding insures tender meat. Use a mallet designed for this purpose. If not available, the resourceful cook grabs a soda bottle and uses the bottom. Be sure to pound enough, but not too much, as pounding can leave the meat limp and unattractive. When I asked Armando the secret of pounding octopus, he said to hold it firmly and swing it against a tree trunk or rock for nine times on one side and then nine times on the other side. There are no guarantees. Practice is the real secret.

Caracol Empanazado—Breaded Deep Fried Conch

Our good friend Dr. Miller, who got us into eco-tourism, always orders this dish. A variation is to use batter instead of the bread crumbs. You can also make small slices and serve like a tempura.

Ingredients:

6 conch, 5–6 oz. each, shelled,
    butterflied, flattened and
    tenderized by pounding
    with a mallet or the bottom
    of a bottle
Salt and pepper
¾ cup unbleached flour
¾ cup fine dry breadcrumbs
1 tsp. crushed oregano
2 eggs, well beaten
Vegetable oil (olive or peanut oil
    are first choice, but any
    other will do) enough for a
    ½-inch depth in the sauté
    pan you are using
6 lime wedges

Preparation:

Lightly salt and pepper the conch
pieces, cover, and refrigerate for half an
hour. Put the flour and the breadcrumbs
mixed with crushed oregano into separate
containers (pie pans are good). Dip the
conch first in the flour, then the egg, and
last in the breadcrumbs. Heat the oil in
a large flying pan and fry the conch until
golden on each side—about 4 minutes.
Drain on toweling and serve immediately
with lime wedges. Serves 6.

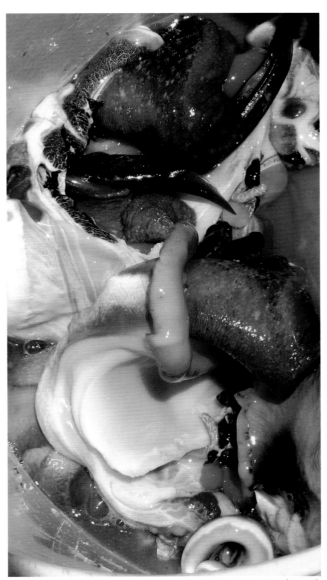

Fresh conch

Batter Fried Conch

Ingredients:

6 conch, 5–6 oz. each, shelled,
butterflied and pounded with
the bottom of a bottle to flatten
and tenderize
1 cup all-purpose flour
2 tsp. vegetable oil
1 tsp. salt
1 cup beer
2 egg whites
6 lime wedges

Preparation:

In a large mixing bowl whisk together the flour, oil, salt and beer. Cover and let stand for at least half an hour. In a separate bowl, whip the whites until they form soft peaks. Fold gently into the batter. In a pan for deep frying heat 1 inch of oil until hot: 375 degrees. Dip the conch into the batter and lower into the hot oil. The pieces will be golden brown on both sides when done. Use tongs to remove conch from the oil and drain on several layers of paper toweling. Serve right away with lime wedges.

Manitos de Cangrejo—Stone Crab Claws

It was at one of Armando's birthday parties away from the beach, where he brought a bushel basket full of stone crabs, that I first had this quick but special meal.

Stone crab meat is very delicate in flavor and texture. Fishermen, after harvesting one claw at a time, return the live crab to its habitat where, barring additional calamity, it will grow another claw. Allow 4 claws or more for each person, depending on the occasion.

Congrejo Asado—Roasted Crab Claws

Put crab claws directly onto hot coals and roast for about 5 minutes, turning once. Crack and serve with lime wedges.

Congrejo al Vapor—Steamed Crab Claws

Fill a large pot with water and bring to a boil adding a teaspoon of salt for each quart of water. If you like, you can throw in a couple of tablespoons of oregano also. Add the crab claws to the water one or two at a time so as not to stop the boiling. Reduce the heat to a simmer and cook for 10 to 15 minutes, or until they turn orange.

Nutcrackers work best to get at the meat. If you want to partially crack the shells before serving, a wooden mallet works better than a hammer because it won't shatter the shells.

Serve with lime wedges. There is no law against melted butter if that appeals to you. Garlic Cream makes a wonderful dip.

Tiburón Asado—Grilled Shark Steaks

Somehow, eating shark instead of being eaten has a great appeal.

Ingredients:
   ½ cup olive oil
   ¼ cup sour orange or a mixture of half
         orange and half lime juice
   2 cloves garlic, minced
   ½ tsp. salt
   ½ tsp. coarsely ground pepper
   4 shark steaks (about 1 ¼ lbs. total) cut
         1 inch thick

Preparation:
   Place the steaks in a glass dish just large enough to hold them. In a small bowl whisk together the olive oil, juice, garlic, salt, pepper and pour over the steaks, turning to coat. Cover loosely and refrigerate for an hour, turning a few times. Prepare hot coals for grilling. When ready, remove the steaks from the marinade and place them in a well-greased grill, 4 inches above the coals. Cook for 8 to 10 minutes turning once with a wide metal spatula. The steaks should be seared on the outside and just cooked through.

Option: Steaks can also be pan grilled in a hot, lightly oiled, heavy skillet.

Mango and Cucumber Salsa are very good with this. Xnipec also goes well, of course.

Maccum—Fish Stew

An adaptation of a traditional clay pot recipe.

Ingredients:
   6 serving-sized, firm, fairly thick, fish
         fillets: snook, grouper, bass,
         snapper, etc. (about 2 lbs.)
   1 cup water
   ¼ cup lime juice or white vinegar
   2 tbsp. achiote paste
   1 tbsp. oregano
   2 bay leaves, crumbled
   1 large white onion, chopped

1 large clove garlic, minced
1 medium bell pepper, diced
4 Roma tomatoes, seeded and diced—or
 enough to make 1 cup

Preparation:

Put the fish in a glass pan large enough to hold the fillets in one layer. Mix together the water and lime juice or vinegar and stir in the achiote paste until dissolved. Pour over the fish and turn pieces to coat well. Sprinkle with salt, oregano, and crumbled bay leaves. Set aside. Heat the oil in a large frying pan and sauté the onion, garlic and bell pepper for about 10 minutes, or until tender. Add the chopped tomato and cook a few minutes longer. Place the marinated fish on top of the onion mixture, adding any remaining marinade to the pan. Bring to a simmer, cover and cook for 10 minutes, turning once. Arrange the fillets on a heated platter, or in individual shallow bowls, and spoon the sauce on top. Serves 6.

Pepe and Armando with octopus catch

Nacho's Escabeche de Pulpo— Nacho's Octopus Escabeche

The octopus we get comes primarily from the Gulf Coast, where fishermen risk their lives in tiny boats when the weather kicks up.

Ingredients:

2 lbs. octopus, cleaned, pounded, and
 cut into small pieces
2 tsp. salt
6 tbsp. olive oil
1 tsp. freshly ground black pepper,
 or to taste
1 head garlic, flame roasted and peeled
1 chile Xcatik or Anaheim or other
 medium hot chile
2 small red onions, sliced into thin
 rounds

2 tsp. cumin, pan toasted and crushed
     in a mortar
1 tbsp. dried oregano, pan toasted
1 bay leaf
½ cup white wine vinegar

Preparation:

Sprinkle the octopus pieces with salt and pepper and let stand a few minutes. Heat the oil in a large frying pan. Add the octopus pieces and cook over high heat, stirring constantly, for 5 minutes. Transfer the octopus together with the accumulated juices to a small deep pot (stainless steel, enamel, or glass). Add the remaining ingredients and enough water to barely cover. Bring to a boil, lower the heat, cover the pot and simmer for 10 minutes. Remove from the heat and let stand at least 2 hours. Before serving take out the garlic, separate, and peel the cloves. Serve in bowls with the octopus, onion and a garlic clove or two in a small pool of broth. Serve warm or at room temperature as an appetizer. Serves 6 to 8.

Ensalada de Calamares—Squid Salad

Don Nacho Jueves, as he likes to be called, is one of the most knowledgeable cooks of regional food I have ever met. Fortunately, I got to work with him and plied him with questions. His answers have strongly influenced this book. Not always a patient man, he sometimes would turn away shaking his head in mild disgust because I had not remembered all the steps to cleaning squid. Other times he would throw his head back with a grunted laugh at my innocence about human nature, but mostly he showed me how to make many a dish when he ran our restaurant and then continued to consult with me. As his sight is failing, he is no longer called upon to season a festival feast but rather to enjoy a few beers and the company. His squid salad was always tender and succulent and I hope yours will be, too.

Ingredients:

2 lbs. small to medium sized squid, tentacles left whole and mantles cut into ½-inch rounds, or, if you prefer, you can use only mantles
1 whole head garlic, flame roasted
1 tbsp. toasted oregano
1 bay leaf
5 peppercorns
½ cup white wine
1 quart water

1 chile Xcatik or Anaheim
1 tbsp. salt
1 tbsp. Dijon mustard
½ cup olive oil
⅓ cup lime juice
1 clove garlic, peeled and crushed
Salt and pepper to taste
¾ pound mixed salad greens
½ small red onion, halved lengthwise
    and cut into slivers
2 tbsp. toasted pumpkin seeds

Preparation:

Tie the whole garlic, oregano, bay leaf and peppercorns together into a piece of cheesecloth. Put it into a pot with the wine, chile Xcatik, salt and water. Bring to a boil, and simmer 10 minutes. Add the squid, bring to a boil again, lower the heat and simmer uncovered for 45 minutes.

While the calamares are cooking, prepare the vinaigrette by putting the mustard in a small bowl and whisking in the olive oil and lime juice and adding the garlic, salt and pepper.

When the calamares are cooked, drain and mix well with all but 3 tbsp. of the vinaigrette and marinate for 2 hours, stirring occasionally. Toss the salad greens with the remaining 3 tablespoons of vinaigrette and arrange on a platter. Top with the marinated calamari and

garnish with the onion slivers, and toasted pumpkin seeds. Serves 6 to 8.

Cooked Octopus ready for ceviche

Pipian de Pescado Asado—Grilled Fish Pipian

Ingredients:

2 lbs. grouper, snapper or bass fillets,
    about 1 inch thick
¼ cup lime juice
Salt and freshly ground pepper
¼ cup vegetable oil
1 recipe Pipian sauce (see page 35)
2 tbsp. cilantro leaves, coarsely chopped
6 lime wedges

Preparation:

Sprinkle the fillets with lime juice, salt, and pepper. Let stand for half an hour. In the meantime, fire up your grill. When the coals have settled down to a medium heat, oil the fish—hands work great for this—and cook the fillets, about 5 minutes on each side. Place the broiled fish in a shallow baking dish, spoon over the Pipian, and bake at 325 degrees for 20 minutes. Carefully transfer the fillets to a heated serving platter. Sprinkle cilantro on the fish and garnish with lime wedges.

Brochetas de Mariscos—Seafood Kebabs

The twist on this brocheta is including plantain on the skewer, adding sweetness to the plate.

Ingredients:

2 lbs. seafood: shrimp, lobster meat, conch, any firm thick fleshed fish (swordfish is especially delicious; bay scallops, though decidedly non-Yucatecan, work very well too)
¼ cup olive oil
¼ cup lime juice
½ tsp. salt, or to taste
2 tsp. freshly ground black pepper
1 ½ tbsp. oregano
2–4 cloves garlic, crushed
6 plum tomatoes, halved lengthwise, or use 12 whole firm cherry tomatoes
1 large green bell pepper, cut into 1 ½ inch squares
1 large red bell pepper, cut into 1 ½ inch squares
1 large white onion, cut in half crosswise and then into 1 inch wedges
1 plantain, slightly underripe, cut into ¾ inch thick rounds

Preparation:

Mix together in a large bowl the ¼ cup oil, lime juice, salt, pepper, oregano and garlic. Add the seafood and stir to coat well. Let stand for an hour. Prepare hot coals for grilling. Thread the seafood and vegetables alternately on six large oiled metal skewers. Oil the grill and cook the kebabs over medium heat for about 5 minutes on each side, basting frequently until done.

Serve right away with Arroz Blanco or Arroz con coco (white rice or rice with coconut). Serves 6.

Escabeche de Calamares—Squid in Escabeche

If you are looking for something new to do with squid, this may be your answer.

Ingredients:

> 1 ½ lbs. Cleaned, small to medium sized squid cut into ½ inch pieces, tentacles left whole
> 2 tsp. pan toasted oregano
> 2 bay leaves
> 1 medium onion, flame roasted and peeled
> 1 head garlic, flame roasted and peeled
> 1 chile Xcatik, flame roasted and peeled
> 1 tsp. freshly ground black pepper
> 1 tsp. salt
> 1 large onion, sliced into crescents about ¼ inch thick
> 1 tbsp. light olive oil
> 4 tbsp. lime juice

Preparation:

Bring a pint of water to a boil and add oregano, bay leaves, roasted onion, garlic, chile, black pepper and salt. Cover and simmer for 10 minutes. Add the squid and additional hot water to cover if necessary and bring to a boil again. Lower the heat and simmer uncovered for 20 minutes. Add the sliced onion, olive oil and lime juice and simmer an additional five minutes. Take out the whole onion and chile. Spoon the Escabeche into bowls, dividing the garlic cloves and onion pieces evenly. Serve with fresh tortillas or hot sliced sweet or sourdough baguettes to dip in the broth. Serves 4.

Pan de Cazón (Shark)—Maya Dagwood Sandwich

This recipe is from Campeche. Prepare the component ingredients ahead of time and put it all together at the last minute for a first course or a late night supper dish. Adding the whole Habanero chile to the tomato sauce is called "letting it walk through the sauce" in Maya thereby imparting the wonderful flavor without the mind-blowing heat.

Ingredients:

> 1 ½ lbs. shark steaks cut 1 inch thick
> Salt to taste
> ¼ cup lime juice
> 1 tbsp. oregano
> 1 tbsp. oil
> 2 lbs. plum tomatoes, roasted
> 1 large white onion, diced
> 2 tbsp. vegetable oil

1 whole chile Habanero or any hot
  green chile
18 3½ to 4 inch corn tortillas
Vegetable oil for frying
1 ½ cups warm frijoles colados
6 small chiles Habaneros, charred and
  left whole

Preparation:

Sprinkle the shark steaks with lime juice, salt, pepper and the oregano. Let them sit while you make the tomato sauce. Blend the tomatoes to a rough purée. Heat the 2 tbsp. oil in a frying pan, add the onion and cook for a minute or so. Add the tomato purée, salt and whole chile and cook until reduced to about 2 cups. Brush the shark steaks with oil and either grill or fry them. Take out any skin and bones and shred finely. Heat a bit of oil in a frying pan. Fry 3 of the tortillas a few moments on each side to soften, then dip into the tomato sauce to just lightly cover and then place one on a heated plate. Spread with a layer of frijoles colados and top with a second tortilla. Spread with a layer of shark and top with the third tortilla. Keep warm in a 200-degree oven and continue until you have completed six plates. Divide the remaining tomato sauce between the six "sandwiches" and top each with a roasted Habanero. Serves 6.

Cazón Entomatato—Shark in Tomato Sauce

Serve this dish with rice and black beans, or use in tacos or as a filling for empañadas.

Ingredients:

1 lb. shark
2 tbsp. lime juice
Salt and pepper to taste
2 tbsp. olive oil
1 cup red onion, chopped
1 clove garlic, minced
¾ lb. Roma tomatoes, peeled, seeded
  and chopped

Preparation:

Cut the shark into ½-inch cubes. Place in a bowl and combine with the lime juice, salt and pepper. Let stand for half an hour, stirring once or twice. Heat the oil in a large frying pan. Cook the onion and garlic until tender. Add the tomatoes and cook for about 5 minutes. Add the shark and cook for another 5 minutes, or until done. The mixture should be fairly dry. If not, turn up the heat to let the excess liquid evaporate. Serves 4.

Shrimp and Pasta Salad

Ingredients:

 1 cup cooked small shrimp
 2 cups cooked rigatoni pasta
 ¼ cup chopped onion
 2 tbsp. chopped chives
 2 hardboiled eggs, chopped
 ¼ cup mayonnaise
 ¼ cup plain yogurt
 Salt and pepper to taste

In a large bowl, combine mayonnaise, yogurt, onions, chives, and shrimp. Add pasta and mix well. Gently fold in hard-boiled eggs. Chill. Serves 4.

Shrimp Chilpachole

Ingredients:

 1 lb. medium shrimp, shelled and
   deveined, the shells reserved
 1 bay leaf
 1 whole dried Guajillo chile
 ½ tsp. salt
 4 whole peppercorns
 2 dried Guajillo chiles, stemmed,
   seeded, deveined, and toasted
 1 tbsp. recado rojo
 ¼ cup very hot water
 ¾ lb. tomatoes
 1 medium onion
 1 large green bell pepper
 4 large cloves garlic, roasted and peeled
 2 tsp. oregano
 2 Chipotle chiles in adobo (canned)
 ½ tsp. ground allspice
 1 tbsp. recado rojo
 ½ tsp. salt
 ½ tsp. freshly ground black pepper
 1 tbsp. chopped epazote, or use cilantro

Preparation:

Put the shrimp shells in a pot with half a cup of water, the bay leaf, Guajillo chile, salt and peppercorns. Bring to a boil, lower the heat. Cover and simmer for 20 minutes. Strain and reserve the stock.

Put the chile pieces and the recado rojo together to soak in ¼ cup of very hot water for half an hour.

In the meantime, roast the tomatoes, onion and bell pepper over a medium flame and put them all together into a paper bag for a few minutes. Take them out, rub off any blackened bits with a paper towel. Seed and chop the tomatoes. Seed, devein and chop the bell pepper, chop the onion and pop the garlic cloves out of their skins.

Put the tomatoes, onion, bell pepper, garlic, Guajillo chiles, recado with hot water, Chipotle chiles, allspice, salt and pepper in a blender and purée for half a minute or so until smooth. Pour into a pot, stir in the shrimp stock and bring to a boil. Add the shrimp and cook just until tender, 3–5 minutes. Serve over rice. Serves 4.

Shrimp with Chiles

If you have ever wondered what to do with excess chiles in the pantry, try this invention.

Ingredients:
    1 lb. large shrimp, shelled and
        deveined
    ⅓ cup vegetable oil
    1–3 Habanero chiles
    4 Xcatik chiles, or substitute any other
        moderately hot chile
    4 Jalapeño chiles
    4 Serrano chiles
    1 small onion, quartered, the pieces
        separated
    3 cloves garlic, crushed
    ½ tsp. salt
    ½ tsp. black pepper
    1 lime, quartered
    Arroz Blanco (see page 127)

Shrimp with Chile Sauce

Preparation:
    Pierce each chile several times with a pointed object to prevent them from exploding in the hot oil. Heat the oil in a large frying pan. Add the chiles, onion, garlic, salt and pepper. Sauté and stir for a few minutes to flavor the oil. The onions and garlic should soften but not brown. Add the shrimp and stir-fry over medium high heat until cooked through, about 5 minutes. Remove the shrimp from the pan. Strain the chile oil over the

cooked rice and stir to mix. Place on a heated platter, top with the shrimp and garnish with some of the chiles. Serve with lime wedges. Serves 4.

Tik In Xik—Painted Fish

This ancient recipe allows for a dramatic presentation of a large whole fish or several smaller ones. The literal translation from Maya refers to an armpit as it hinges open, as does the butterflied fish presented here. Make the butterfly by cutting the scaled and gutted fish along the spine on one side and gently separating the meat from the bone until it spreads open. Score the flesh in diagonals to enhance the penetration of the achiote marinade.

Imagine the Maya arriving on the white sand beaches of Quintana Roo in dugout canoes, building campfires to cook their freshly caught fish entwined with achiote paste.

The many varieties of groupers are all members of that large family of fish known as sea bass. Our Caribbean grouper tastes much like lobster and is superb. Red snapper can also be prepared to very good effect with this recipe. Grill over coals as the ancients did.

Tik In Xik, Painted Fish

Ingredients:

1 whole grouper or other whole bass, or
    red snapper, approximately 5 lbs.
4 tbsp. recado rojo
4 large cloves garlic, minced
1 tbsp. salt
2 tsp. pepper
½ cup lime juice
2 large white onions, thinly sliced
4 tomatoes, thinly sliced

Preparation:

Mix the achiote paste with the garlic, salt, pepper and lime juice. Rub the mixture over the fish and top with the onion and tomato slices. Let stand while you fire up the grill or heat oven for half an hour if you are baking the fish. The general rule is to cook the fish for 10 minutes per inch for thickness. If you are baking, use a 450-degree oven, place fish in a baking pan and fashion a tent of aluminum foil to cover. However you do it, place this beautiful and dramatic creation on a heated platter in the center of the table and let people slice portions for themselves with a sharp knife. Serves 6 to 8.

Note: A simple option is to use fillets of any firm white fish, marinate for 20 minutes and then bake or grill.

Sac Kai—White Fish

Prepare fish as for Tik in Xik, but omit the recado rojo and use only garlic, salt and pepper and lime juice for seasoning. Serve in the same manner.

Fish and Rice Salad

Ingredients:
>   1 cup cooked fish, flaked (use any firm, white fleshed fish)
>   2 cups cooked white rice
>   ¼ cup chopped green onions
>   ¼ cup chopped green pepper
>   ¼ cup cilantro, finely chopped
>   ¾ cup olive oil
>   ¼ cup lime juice
>   Salt and pepper

Preparation:
In a medium sized bowl, mix the rice, fish, green onions, green pepper and cilantro. Whisk together the olive oil and lime juice, add to the bowl and toss lightly to combine. Add salt and pepper to taste. Serves 4.

Bare handed catch of snapper by Armando

7

THE BASICS

Monte

The ancient Maya offered miniature *manos* and metates (mortar and pestle) in rituals to the rain gods. The planting stick and machete aid men in the ageless task of survival and growing corn in the jungle. Beans and rice are at the heart of the Maya meal and sometimes are the meal itself.

For centuries, the monte, or forest jungle, on the Quintana Roo coast has provided subsistence hunting and trapping for the Maya. On an expedition into the monte, a *campesino* took his ever-present machete, water, and corn or corn flour. The trip into the monte was often on foot, with mule trains carrying out the game, tropical hardwoods, and chicle extracted from the *zapote* trees.

It is said that the Wrigley brothers made their chewing gum fortune from chicle harvested by the Maya of Quintana Roo. Today, the market for chicle is practically nonexistent. Because of the lengthy trips, arduous harvests, laborious processing, and the

113

current low return, few *chicleros* remain. However, along the highway you can often see machete scars high on zapote trees from which chicle has been extracted.

The tough men of the monte, and the courageous women who went along to cook, often encountered wild boar, pit vipers, peccary, jaguars, ocelotes, tepesquintle, wild turkey, quail, *chachalaca*, rabbits, wild duck, fire ants, and iguanas. A few of these later became *guisados*, or regional dishes.

Maya Pax

When I heard my first words of Maya conversation, they sounded like Japanese to me. Then when I first heard Maya music, it sounded like mountain music of the Appalachians. I was in a remote forest village, Kopchen, to buy hand woven baskets the villagers make to sell. In a front room shop in someone's home, I surveyed the symmetry (or lack thereof) in the weave of a large covered basket. This person spoke Spanish as well as Maya, so we were able to communicate.

As we talked, I heard a drum and handmade wooden fiddle begin to play on a knoll about 100 yards away. The rhythmic melodies flowed from a small building, the local Maya church. Everyone was required to take off shoes

The Painted Fish and Other Mayan Feasts

before entering and bow down before an altar complete with candles, icons, and flowers.

There were three male musicians as is the custom for Maya Pax music. One plays the violin and the two others each perform on handmade snare drums devised by the skillful use of machetes to hollow out tree trunks. The larger of the two is called a Bombo and the smaller is a Tarola. Both are topped and secured with goat skin.

Another interesting instrument is made from the jícara, which is gourd-like but grows on a tree. Hollowed out it is used either as a musical instrument or as a bowl to serve atole (see following note). Often decorated with carvings of animals and local scenes, it is hit by small wooden hammers and played like a marimba.

Atole—Corn Porridge

At our ranch, Don Jose often dilutes masa harina to make *atole*, a refreshing drink, to give him energy. Many Maya men drink atole while away from home working their milpa, or subsistence farm.

Atole can be eaten hot or cold. Prepare by diluting corn dough in hot water and bringing it to a boil. Simmer until thickened and well cooked. Atole should have the consistency of a thin sauce.

DOÑA PAOLA

Felipe Carrillo Puerto,
Quintana Roo
March 30, 1990

Doña Paola died last night. By eight this morning, family and friends gathered in her home.

Colorful bouquets of bougainvillea, baby's breath, flamboyant and maidenhair fern surrounded the open casket. Standing candelabras with colored electric lights accentuated the corners of the box that held her frail old body. A matching crucifix was on a tripod. A green light lit the head of the casket, contrasting with the magenta petals of bougainvillea that crowned the crucified Christ just below the light.

Lela, one of Doña Paola's daughters, was visibly grieving. She occupied herself lighting candles on a table in the corner of the crowded room. The women sat silently on chairs around the periphery of the small room. The men stayed outside, standing and talking quietly. Friends of the family served coffee and soft drinks.

I sat and mused about my many encounters with Doña Paola during my previous seven years as her neighbor in Punta Allen. She always called me "Soñita," as though I were a young girl. I will miss her strong hugs and her wisdom.

Sobados Modernos

Maya massage is highly valued for sprained ankles, stiff backs, and to sooth pregnant women. I first experienced it for a pulled back muscle. While I was having a pedicure, I asked those in my friend Paola's *estética* (beauty salon) who could help me. Everyone firmly agreed that Doña Carmela was the best in town, but that she was often too busy to take new clients.

Luckily, I caught Doña Carmela at a free moment, and she took me into her workspace—a room of her thatch roofed home. The walls were stucco, and a curtain hung to the floor as a partition. She spread a thick blanket on the concrete floor and asked me to lie down on it on my stomach. She worked deeply into muscles in an organized, practiced manner, bringing me to the edge of (and sometimes all the way past) my pain threshold.

Before I got up, after she finished, she asked me if I had a *rebozo*, or shawl. I said I did, but not with me. She softly offered to loan me one and asked me to stand up. As I rose and looked at her creased, perspiring face, I realized that this ferociously strong woman—who had just bent to the floor and sometimes balanced on her knees as she massaged my aching body—must be nearly 90 years old.

Doña Carmela wrapped me tightly in the rebozo and gave me instructions to go home and sleep and drink a lot of water. As I left, I passed by her waiting clients—all pregnant women. They had come for abdominal massages and perhaps a realignment of the umbilical cord. This is done by localizing a pulse in the abdomen and moving it to its proper place.

Young mothers come regularly to Doña Carmela at very little cost. She is the *madrona*, or midwife, so she knows each mother and will already know the child when it arrives.

Doña Feliciana, another friend, is studying to become a midwife and learning to give information to her community about birth control. She also works with her mother, who has been a madrona for 39 years and has delivered most of the people in her village. Although Doña Feliciana has no birth certificate, we believe that she is at least 50, so her mother is well along in years. Doña Feliciana's mother is teaching her the older customs of childbirth, in which the birth

takes place in a hammock. I was fascinated when I realized that my husband was born in a hammock—while my Finnish mother was born in a rural Finnish sauna.

Ranchito—Small Ranch

This morning the air was unusually cool when we made our seven a.m., two-kilometer hike in to our new ranch in the Zona Maya of Quintana Roo. I felt my lungs effortlessly enjoying the fresh early morning air. Armando and I each carried a kilo of warm tortillas under one arm. We had promised to bring them to the workers living on the ranch.

Even going at a brisk pace, we saw many birds and heard many more. There were chachalakas, mot-mots, Yucatán parrots,

Yucatán jays, toucans, cardinals and mourning doves. We smelled the odor of jaguar in the same area as yesterday but this time we saw its tracks. It had been scratching at the roosting place of four wild turkeys very close to our entrance gate.

On the return hike, we saw a half-eaten tropical wild fruit, *chicozapote*. Armando suggested that it had been left behind by a tepesquintle, a member of the rodent family that savors those fruits. Tepesquintle, called

Paca in English, have large back haunches, stubby faces and light brown fur with white spots. A local delicacy, they are skinned and marinated in sour orange juice, bathed in recado rojo, then wrapped in banana leaves and cooked in a pit on coals. Maya families often sell this critter by holding it up to passing motorists on route 307 between Tulum and Felipe Carrillo Puerto. You could try this food of the ancient Maya gods, but check the feet for positive identification.

Author with Suegro's horse

The Painted Fish and Other Mayan Feasts

SOUPS

If you were to hold a *junto secreto* (secret meeting), it would have to end before the rooster crows at around four a.m., because that is when the Maya morning officially begins. The roosters in town must be confused, because they often crow at the false dawn of two a.m., much to the displeasure of some of our guests. After being woken several nights in a row, one of our guests wanted to put a "contract" out on the neighbor's rooster for just such behavior. Armando commented with disbelief, "*Está natural*" (it is natural).

Chicken stock

Ingredients:
   1 ½ cups water, or use canned chicken
      broth if the neck, wing tips and
      feet are not included with your
      chicken
   Pieces of one chicken
   1 whole clove
   1 whole allspice
   2 whole peppercorns
   a clove of garlic
   a few slices of carrot
   a pinch of salt

Preparation:
   Bring to a boil, skim, and cook for about 15 minutes until reduced by a third. Strain.

Sopa de Frijoles Negros—Black Bean Soup

Black bean soup is so satisfying it can serve as a light lunch with crusty French bread. Remember to serve plenty of cilantro and chopped raw onion on the side.

Black bean soup

Ingredients:

- ½ lb. black beans, cooked (see basic black bean recipe, page 130)
- Broth from the beans, plus water to make 4 cups
- Pinch of powdered chile Piquin or Cayenne pepper
- Salt to taste
- 4 corn tortillas, halved, cut into strips and fried crisp in ¼ inch hot oil
- ½ cup white onion, minced
- ¼ cup cilantro, chopped
- ¼ cup fresh mint, chopped
- 1 lime, quartered

Preparation:

Put the beans and liquid into a 3-quart pot. Bring to a boil, lower the heat and simmer for 30 minutes, stirring occasionally. Add chile Piquin or Cayenne and salt to taste. Divide the tortilla strips between heated soup bowls. Ladle the soup into the bowls, serve, and pass individual dishes of onion, cilantro, mint and lime. Serves 4 to 6.

Capi's Caldo

Cappy was a sea captain. He is a fine coastal cook who owns a coconut ranch that I had the good fortune to visit when the copra (coconut) industry of the peninsula was prospering. With a hundred years of warning, the lethal yellowing disease has now closed down 90% of the active coconut ranches. However, a resistant strain, the Malaysian dwarf coconut, has been planted and has begun producing. Capi's ranch kitchen is orderly and clean like a ship's galley. He uses a self-made tool to shave the coconut meat. His skill with a machete is exacting, whether it be harvesting a coconut or serving one for drinking. It is from him and his family that I learned much about Mexican hospitality. It is worth it to make the coconut milk, which gives a distinctive yet delicate flavor to Capi's *caldo*.

Ingredients:

- 1 fresh coconut
- 4 serving sized red snapper fillets (approximately 1 lb.)
- 1 large garlic clove, sliced in thin rounds
- 1 small white onion, finely chopped
- 2 tbsp. chopped cilantro (optional)
- 1 lime, cut into 4 wedges

Preparation:

First, make the coconut milk. To do this, pierce the three eyes with an ice pick and bake the coconut in a 350-degree oven for 20 minutes. Then place it on a solid surface and give it a few whacks with a hammer to break it up into large pieces. Take the meat from the shell, pare off the brown skin and grate it in a food processor with a little cold water. Add 3 cups scalding water and process for half a minute or so. Let the coconut mixture stand for 15 minutes and then strain, pressing down on the meat with a wooden spoon to extract as much flavor as possible.

Measure the coconut milk and add enough water to make 3 cups. Pour it into a shallow pot large enough to hold the fish in a single layer. Heat it to a simmer and add the fish and, if necessary, additional water to cover. Add garlic and onion. Simmer until the fish is translucent and separates easily from the bone. Serve in shallow bowls with lime wedges. Serves 4.

Sopa de Caracol—Conch Soup

The name of this recipe is the title of a very popular song a few years past. I seldom can get the refrain out of my head when ordering this very rich and filling soup.

Ingredients:
    1 ½ lbs. conch meat, pounded and cut
        into small cubes
    2 tbsp. lemon juice
    Salt
    2 tbsp. olive oil
    1 medium onion, diced
    3 cloves garlic, minced
    1 small red bell pepper, diced
    1 chayote, peeled, pitted, and cut into ½
        inch cubes (optional)
    4 Roma tomatoes, seeded and diced
    2 medium red potatoes, peeled and cut
        into ½-inch cubes
    1 ½ quarts water
    1 tsp. freshly ground black pepper
    1 tsp. dried oregano
    1 tbsp. cilantro, chopped
    6 lime wedges
    Simple Habanero Chile Salsa or Salsa
        Tamulado

Preparation:
Sprinkle the conch with lemon juice and salt. Toss to coat evenly and set aside. Heat the olive oil in a soup pot and sauté the onion until soft. Add the garlic, chayote, and tomato, and sauté for an additional five minutes. Add the conch, water, pepper and oregano. Bring to a boil and simmer, covered, for 10 minutes. Add the potatoes and cook another 10 minutes, or until the potatoes are tender. Ladle into heated bowls, sprinkle with cilantro and serve with lime wedges. Pass salsa separately. Serves 6.

Chayote Soup

Puréeing the chayote gives a delicious texture and color to this light soup.

Ingredients:

    4 medium chayotes, peeled, cut into
        quarters and pitted
    4 cups water
    1 tbsp. olive oil
    ½ cup chopped onion
    ¼ cup chopped green bell pepper
    1 tbsp. chopped garlic
    2 large Roma tomatoes, seeded,
        cored and chopped
    1 tsp. salt
    ¼ tsp. pepper
    1 cup half-and-half
    Small amount of minced fresh
        chives or flat leaf parsley
        for the top

Preparation:

Place the chayotes in a medium large pot with water. Cover and bring to a boil. Lower the heat and simmer, covered, until very tender (about 15 minutes). In the meantime, heat the oil in a small skillet. Add the onion and sauté for about 5 minutes. Add the green bell pepper, the garlic, and the tomato and continue to cook, covered, over low heat for another 10 minutes until the vegetables are very soft. Using a food processor or a blender, purée the chayote and its liquid with the sautéed vegetable mixture. Do this in several small batches to avoid messy overflow. Transfer the purée to the original saucepan, add the salt and pepper, and reheat. Add the half-and-half and bring to a simmer. Taste and add more salt and pepper if you like. Serve hot, topped with fresh herbs. Serves 4 to 6.

Chayotes

Sopa de Ajo—Garlic Soup

I still remember clearly my first lesson in making garlic soup. The day was unusually bright with a golden light as I entered the dark kitchen of one of the most curious places on the beaches of Quintana Roo, Mexico: Kai Lu'um. There the mestiza cook, Lupita, dressed in a colorful huipil, deftly reproduced both regional and "foreign food" with an unusual skill and openness. The final gesture to finish this soup caught in my memory; raise the arms high and drizzle in the beaten eggs to create an egg drop finish.

This soup is a must for garlic lovers all over the world.

Fresh Garlic

Ingredients:

    4 tbsp. olive oil
    2 tbsp. minced garlic, or even 4,
        depending on your predilection
    1 medium white onion, chopped
    3 plum tomatoes, seeded, cored and
        diced
    6 cups rich chicken broth
    1 egg, lightly beaten
    Salt and pepper to taste
    Croutons (see below)

Preparation:

Heat the oil in a small skillet. Have ready a strainer placed in a 3-quart saucepot. Sauté the garlic until it is golden, and then scrape it into the strainer letting the oil drain into the pot. Reserve the garlic. Sauté the onion in the garlic oil until soft, about 10 minutes. Add the diced tomato and cook a few minutes longer. Add the chicken broth and the reserved garlic, bring the soup to a boil, lower the heat to a simmer and cook, covered, for 15 minutes. Add salt and freshly ground pepper to taste.

Just before serving, drizzle in the beaten egg while stirring constantly with a wooden spoon to create "egg drops." Ladle into bowls and top each serving with a crouton.

Croutons: cut ¼-inch crosswise slices from a baguette style loaf of French bread. Brush with olive oil and place on a baking sheet. Toast in a moderate oven, turning once, until golden brown on both sides. Serves 4 to 6.

Gazpacho Rojo—Red Gazpacho

The Spaniards brought this cold vegetable soup, which we often prefer on a humid summer day.

Ingredients:

    1 quart tomato juice
    1 medium red or green bell pepper,
        coarsely chopped
    1 medium onion, coarsely chopped
    1 medium cucumber, peeled, seeded and
        coarsely chopped
    3 cloves garlic, finely chopped
    1 Serrano chile, seeds and veins
        removed, minced
    2 tbsp. lemon juice
    2 tbsp. wine vinegar (white, red, or
        sherry)
    3 tbsp. virgin olive oil

    ½ tsp. salt
    ½ tsp. freshly ground black pepper
    Garnish:
    1 large Roma tomato, peeled, seeded
        and cut into small cubes
    2 tbsp. chives, sliced thin
    2 ½ inch thick white bread slices,
        crusts removed and diced small,
        sautéed over medium high heat
        in a little oil until golden and
        drained on paper toweling.

Preparation:

Purée the vegetables in a blender or a food processor, adding just enough of the tomato juice to keep the blades from clogging and leaving some texture to the mixture. Pour into a large bowl and mix in the remaining tomato juice, the lemon juice, vinegar, olive oil, salt and pepper. Cover and chill for several hours until very cold. Stir and taste, adding more salt, pepper, lemon or lime juice and vinegar to taste. Ladle into bowls and top with diced tomato, chives, and bread cubes. Serves 4 to 6.

Potaje de Lentejas—Lentil Soup

This hardy dish serves as a fine lunch. The ingredients can vary according to what is on hand but cooking bananas are a must for authentic flavor. Doña Feliciana, the señora that helps me in my home, likes to make the deluxe version and often asks me to buy all the ingredients for her to make it. However, if some items are missing, she cheerfully makes it anyway. Making a large pot of *potaje* is preferred as its flavor improves the second day. You should have at least one to two cupfuls left over. I recommend putting the leftovers in the blender to make a delicious dip to be eaten with tostados as a botana.

Ingredients:

    6 cups water
    1 ½ cups lentils
    1 onion, chopped
    2 carrots, cubed
    2 turban or buttercup squash—choose
        small squash with tender shiny
        skin
    1 large potato, cubed
    2 medium sweet potatoes, peeled, cubed
    1 chayote, pitted and cubed
    2 plantains (cooking bananas) sliced in
        rounds with skin on (this holds
        the shape nicely)
    1 chile Xcatik or any medium hot chile,
        whole (optional)
    Salt and pepper to taste

Preparation:

Put the ingredients except the plantains and salt and pepper into a pot, bring to a boil, cover and simmer for 45 minutes or until the lentils are tender but still hold their shape. Add salt, pepper, and the sliced plantains and cook for an additional 10 minutes. Remove the whole chile and ladle into bowls. Remove banana skins before eating. Serves 6.

Sopa de Lima

Mexico has various types of limes; there is no lemon, as we know it. The limes and other citrus provide surprisingly savory marinades and garnishes. This soup calls for *"limas"* which have a blander, whiter pulp than the lime, which I suggest using as a substitute. It is a different flavor, but it is citrus and reminiscent of the lima. Use no juice. Float slices on the soup to impart a marked flavor on the broth.

Ingredients:

    1 large whole chicken breast, skin
        removed
    6 cups water
    1 white onion, chopped
    2 tomatoes, seeded and chopped
    1 tbsp. oil

Salt and pepper to taste
½ lb. stale tortillas, cut into narrow
  strips (or take fresh ones, cut
  them up and spread them out to
  dry a bit)
Additional vegetable oil for frying
1 lemon or lime, cut into thin rounds

Preparation:

Put the chicken breast, water, salt and pepper into a 3-quart pot. Bring to a boil, lower the heat and skim off any foam. Cover and simmer for 30 minutes. Take out the chicken breast and set aside to cool. Heat 1 tbsp. oil in a frying pan and sauté the onion and tomato until soft. Add to the chicken broth and cook for 20 minutes. While the soup is cooking, pour oil to a depth of ½ inch into a medium sized frying pan. Heat until just below the smoking point—very hot—and fry the tortilla strips in batches (do not crowd the pan), adding additional oil as necessary. Drain on paper toweling. Remove the bone from the breast and cut the meat up into bite sized pieces. Add the chicken and lime slices to the pot for the last two minutes of cooking. Ladle into heated bowls, dividing the meat evenly and including a lime slice with each serving. Top with fried tortilla strips. Serves 4 to 6.

Seafood Stock

To make an especially rich stock, take 1 quart fish or chicken broth and add shells of lobster and/or shrimp, and cook down to about 3 cups.

Sopa de Mariscos

Also a meal in itself, this soup is flexible, using many of the ingredients that you have on hand. I call it Maya Bouillabaisse.

Ingredients:

1 boneless, skinless fish fillet (about ½
  lb.), cut into 1-inch cubes
2 lbs. Shellfish: lobster, crab, shrimp,
  scallops—the more variety the
  better—shelled and cut into bite
  sized pieces
Juice of 1 lemon
Salt to taste
2 tbsp. olive oil
2 medium onions, chopped
6 Roma tomatoes, seeded and diced
6 cups fish stock or 2 cups clam juice
  and 4 cups water
2 tbsp. cilantro, chopped (optional)
6 lime wedges
Habanero Chile Salsa or Salsa Tamulado

Preparation:

Sprinkle the fish with lemon juice and salt and set aside. Heat the oil in a large heavy pot. Add the onions and cook until they are soft. Add the tomatoes and cook 2 or 3 minutes longer. Add the stock or clam juice and water, and the fish. Bring to a boil, lower the heat, and simmer a few minutes until done. Take care not to overcook. Ladle into heated bowls and sprinkle with cilantro if desired. Serve each bowl with a lime wedge and pass salsa separately. Serves 4 to 6.

Basic ingredients

VEGETABLES, BEANS AND RICE

Arroz Blanco—White Rice

Ingredients:
> 1 cup long-grain white rice
> 1 tbsp. oil
> ¼ cup minced onion
> 1 clove garlic, peeled and crushed with
> > the broad side of a knife blade
> ½ tsp. salt
> 2 cups water

Preparation:

Heat the oil in a pot. Add the onion and garlic and sauté for a few minutes until the onions are soft. Add the rice and stir well. Add the water and bring to a boil. Stir, cover, lower the heat and cook for 15 minutes or until done. Turn off the heat and let the rice stand for 5 minutes, then fluff with a fork. Serves 4.

Note: White Basmati rice works very well in this and the following rice recipes.

Arroz con Coco y Frijoles Negros—Coconut Rice with Black Beans

This is a murky-looking, very tasty dish that is much liked throughout the Caribbean.

Ingredients:

>   1 tbsp. oil
>   1 cup long-grain white rice
>   1 ½ cups coconut milk
>   ½ tsp. salt
>   1 ½ cups black beans, cooked,
>   with their liquid

Preparation:

Heat the oil in a heavy skillet. Add the rice and sauté, stirring, for 5 minutes. Add the coconut milk (you should have enough to cover the rice with an extra ¼ inch on top). Add the salt and stir. Add the beans with their liquid and stir well again. Bring to a boil over medium heat. Turn the heat to very low, cover the pot and simmer until the rice is tender, about 15 minutes. Stir gently before serving. Serves 4 to 6.

Arroz con Coco—Coconut Rice

Ingredients:

>   1 cup long grain white rice
>   2 cups coconut milk
>   3 tbsp. minced white onion
>   1 large clove garlic, peeled and crushed
>   with the broad side of a knife
>   ½ tsp. salt

Preparation:

Bring the coconut milk slowly to a boil in a large pot. Add the onion, garlic, rice and salt. Stir, lower the flame and cover. Let cook without stirring for 20 to 25 minutes, or until tender. Turn off the heat and let stand 5 minutes and then stir with a fork to fluff. Serves 4.

Calabasa Frita—Sautéed Squash

Small, shiny, dark green turban squash are preferred, but any other firm squash can be used. This is a basic vegetable recipe often served as a botana with tostadas.

Ingredients:

>   2 tbsp. vegetable oil
>   1 medium white onion, diced
>   1 diced green bell pepper

2 garlic cloves, minced
3 medium tomatoes, seeded and diced
4 small turban or buttercup squash,
      chopped.
2 tbsp. water

Preparation:

Heat the oil in a sauté pan. Add the onion, bell pepper and garlic and cook until tender. Add the diced tomatoes, the squash and the water. Stir, cover and cook for about 15 minutes or until tender. Serve warm or at room temperature. Serves 4.

Chayotes Capeados—Breaded Chayote

These pear-shaped vegetables often stump the best of cooks. Its mild flavor is accented by seasoned toppings.

Ingredients:

1 lb. chayote (about 2 medium)
2 eggs
1 cup fine, dry bread crumbs
1 tsp. dried oregano
1 tsp. salt
1 tsp. pepper
Oil

Preparation:

Cut the *chayote*, including the seed, into even crosswise slices about ½ inch thick. In a small bowl, whisk the eggs together until very well mixed.

Mix the bread crumbs, oregano, salt and pepper and turn out into a pie pan or a plate. Dip the chayote slices in the beaten eggs and then coat with the seasoned bread crumbs. Set aside on a piece of waxed paper or plastic wrap. Heat oil (a depth of ¼ inch) until medium hot. Fry the chayote until golden brown on both sides, turning once with tongs (about 2 minutes for each side). Serves 4.

Homegrown Chayote

Frijoles Negros—Black Beans: Basic Recipe

Armando once said, "It is not a meal without black beans and they are not black beans without epazote." These are "Maya secretos" (Mayan secrets) I would like to share:

Do not add the epazote or the salt until the skins on the beans are tender from cooking. Otherwise, they will not absorb the flavor.

If, while cooking, it is necessary to add more water, add only hot or warm water. Addition of cold water will cause the skins to stay tough forever.

Ingredients:

1 lb. black beans
2 ½ quarts cold water
2 tbsp. oil
1 medium onion, chopped
1 clove garlic, peeled and crushed
1 tbsp. salt
¼ cup fresh epazote, chopped,
      or 1 tbsp. dried

Preparation:

Put the beans and (cold) water in a large pot. Bring to a boil and skim off any starchy foam that rises to the top. Lower the heat and add the oil, onion and garlic. Cover the pot and simmer until the beans are very tender, 1 to 2 hours. Add the salt and epazote and cook for another 15 minutes. It is customary to serve the beans with some of their liquid. Serves 8 to 10.

Basic Black Beans

Frijoles Colados—Strained Beans

The traditional preparation of *Frijoles Colados* involves peeling the beans individually by rubbing them between the fingers, then forcing the bean pulp through a strainer, adding the cooking broth to facilitate the process. The food processor eliminates much tedium. You can also use a blender or, better yet if you happen to have one, a food mill. The consistency can be from soup-like to a creamy purée, depending on how you plan to use them.

Ingredients:
    1 recipe cooked black beans
    ¼ cup oil
    ½ cup minced onion
    1 whole chile Habanero
    Salt to taste

Preparation:
    Drain the beans, reserving the broth. Purée in batches, adding enough broth to make a smooth purée. Heat the oil in a large heavy pot. Add the onion and sauté until tender. Add the bean purée and enough additional broth to achieve the desired consistency. Heat to a simmer, stirring constantly. Turn the heat to very low and add the whole chile Habanero. Cover and cook for half an hour, stirring often and adding additional broth as necessary. Remove the chile and add salt to taste. You can set aside however much you want for immediate use and freeze the rest in ½ to 1 pint containers.

Frijoles Blancos—White Beans

Seasonally we have white beans called "Ibis" that provide a pleasant change from our daily black bean ritual. Use great northern beans for a similar effect and follow the basic bean recipe above. Garnish with chopped cilantro and onion.

Papas con Cilantro, Ajo y Lima—Potatoes with Cilantro, Garlic and Lime

Ingredients:
    1 lb. small red potatoes
    2 tbsp. olive oil
    1 tbsp. minced garlic
    2 tbsp. lime juice
    Salt and freshly ground black pepper
    ¼ cup coarsely chopped cilantro

Preparation:
    Cook the potatoes in salted water just until tender. Drain, cool, peel and cut into halves or quarters, depending on the size. Heat the oil in a frying pan. Add the garlic and cook for a minute or so, then add the potatoes. Cook, turning with a spatula or large spoon, until slightly browned. Add lime juice, salt, pepper and cilantro. Serves 4.

Ensalada de Repollo—Cabbage Salad

Doña Gena, who helped in our restaurant kitchen for a couple of years, deftly shredded cabbage with a sharp knife by working on the edges of a large head, slowly turning it to maintain the finely cut leaf size. Dousing the cabbage with hot water takes the bite out of the raw cabbage but leaves the flavor. Known as one of the best vegetables to eat for one's health, use cabbage as a salad to replace lettuce, limited in the Yucatán to a leafy variety that wilts quickly and offers no crunch.

Ingredients:

    2 cups shredded white cabbage
    3 plum tomatoes, diced
    3 tbsp. finely chopped red onion
        (optional)
    4 tbsp. lime juice or white vinegar
    3 tbsp. cilantro, finely chopped
    Seeded and minced Habanero chile to
        taste: ½ to 2 tsp.
    ½ tsp. salt

Preparation:

    Put the cabbage in a heatproof bowl. Pour over it 1 ½ cups boiling water and let stand for a couple of minutes. Drain in a colander and run cold water over it. Squeeze the water from the cabbage and place in a bowl. Add the tomatoes, lime juice, cilantro, chile and salt. Mix well and serve. Serves 4 to 6.

Ensalada de Doña Gloria—Doña Gloria's Pickled Vegetables

Ingredients:

    1 small red onion, peeled, cut
        lengthwise and sliced into
        crescents
    2 tbsp. white vinegar
    1 tsp. (or more) seeded, minced chile
        Habanero
    1 tbsp. fresh oregano, chopped, or 1 tsp.
        dried
    Pinch of sugar
    Salt to taste
    2 medium red potatoes, peeled and cut
        into ¾ inch cubes
    2 medium carrots, peeled and cut
        crosswise into ½ in thick slices

Preparation:

    Blanch the onion by placing it in a colander and pouring boiling water over. Let drain and put into a bowl with the vinegar, Habanero, oregano, sugar and salt. Let stand while you cook the red potatoes and carrots just until tender and drain them. Mix all the ingredients together and chill, stirring from time to time. Serves 4.

Chaya

There is a plant that grows in the backyard of most Maya homes that provides the necessary "green" in the Maya diet. Considered a bush, the leggy stalks produce a deep green-veined, wide leaf that should be harvested early in the morning while the dew is still evident. This is supposed to keep its miniscule barbs from piercing the harvesters' skin as it is gathered by pulling the underside of a leaf to break it. I have had no luck with this technique and gratefully accept already picked leaves to cook or make into a green drink. *Chaya* can be compared to spinach but definitely has a different flavor. It is an ancient plant easily propagated by snapping off a stalk from the mother plant and sticking it into the earth. Because of its sturdy character, it has survived for centuries and is considered a valuable food during famine. Its deep green leaves are plentiful, flavorful and known to have significant protein and vitamins.

As a beverage, it is blended with water and a squirt of lime juice and is used as a palliative for kidney problems.

Alone, chaya can be sautéed or steamed or combined with onions, tomatoes, garlic, or bacon and served as you would spinach.

Potatoes with Chaya

Though chaya is not likely to be available unless you happen to have a chaya shrub in your yard, this dish is also very good made with spinach.

Ingredients:
> 1 lb. red potatoes
> 2 tbsp. olive oil
> 1 tbsp. minced garlic
> ¼ cup chopped red onion
> 1 bunch spinach or chard, stemmed,
>   washed, dried and cut crosswise
>   into 1-inch strips
> Salt and freshly ground pepper to taste

Preparation:
Cook the potatoes in salted water just until tender. Drain, cool, peel or not, and cut into quarters. Meanwhile, heat the olive oil and sauté the garlic and onion until tender. Add the potatoes and mix carefully. Add the spinach or chard and cook briefly, stirring, until done. Do not overcook. Serves 4.

8

CELEBRATIONS OF LIFE

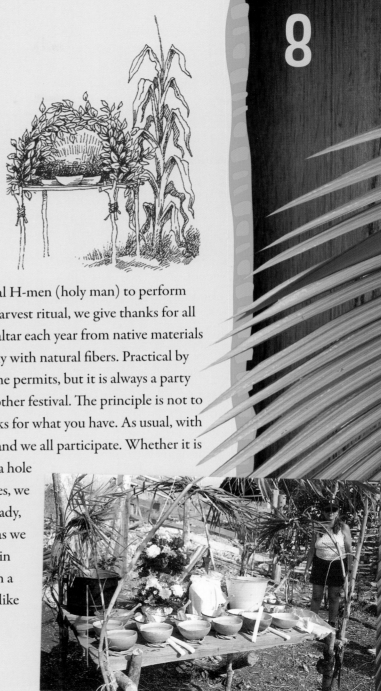

La Primicia—The First Fruit

Rancho el Angel is a subsistence farm with interpretive trails through the jungle for visitors and tourists. Each year we call upon our local H-men (holy man) to perform a thanksgiving ceremony at our ranch. Primarily a harvest ritual, we give thanks for all we enjoy from the ranch. The H-men builds a new altar each year from native materials he finds at our site, tying the decorative altar securely with natural fibers. Practical by nature, Armando schedules this ceremony when time permits, but it is always a party unto itself and never combined with a birthday or other festival. The principle is not to worry about what you do not have but to give thanks for what you have. As usual, with celebrations, the preparations are part of the ritual and we all participate. Whether it is clearing the land for the H-men's new altar, digging a hole for a pit oven, slaughtering a turkey or washing dishes, we enjoy each other's company. When the H-men is ready, we gather and quietly feel the earth under our feet as we sense gratitude for all we have. After sacred prayers in Maya by the H-men, we taste the offerings served in a halved jícara (gourd), and the day continues much like any other happy gathering with music and feasting.

135

Birth

Within weeks of the birth of his son, our friend and neighbor Lupe invited us and other friends to a celebration feast at his house. His wife and sisters are expert makers of flour tortillas, which are not usually served in this region.

What better occasion than the birth of a son to share a venison dish with a historical past! A pit was prepared and lighted, the wood fuel heating the surrounding rocks. Meanwhile, deer meat was marinated in achiote and sour orange, then placed in a long, wide pan (1 ½ by 3 feet) lined with banana leaves. More banana leaves were placed on top of the venison, the pan was lowered into the pit and covered with hot rocks from the fire. Later on, the venison-filled soft taco delights seemed to vanish.

The Mexican government has been very farsighted in granting permission to certain communities to continue their subsistence hunting of deer, as has been the custom for centuries.

Semana Santa

I will always remember the year that Armando's family promised to bring food supplies with them when they came for Easter week. At that time, no *tiendas* (stores) in town stocked meat or produce. Still, it seemed redundant to say they would bring food since they never travel without some offering from their kitchens. Usually they brought tamales wrapped in banana leaves as these travel well. Sometimes corn bread, baked tostadas, recados, or even chocolomo were transported to the beach.

This visit being for all of Easter week, family members arrived in caravan direct from Tizimin, Yucatán. As the smiling children climbed down from the back of pick-up trucks, they shouted "*Tia*! *Tio*!" (Aunt, Uncle) and raced to give us each a big hug and kiss. As I straightened from the last hug with a three year old, I saw a live *borrego*, or lamb, unleashed from the bed of one of the trucks. Coaxed down and tied to a tree in the shade, the lamb thirstily drank offered water. The usual family "hanging out" ensued while everyone prepared sustenance, had a few drinks and shared life stories. Snorkeling trips on the brilliant reef and fishing trips with sparkling water cascading from jumping barracuda became the seeds of stories for future gatherings. These preliminary ways of being together are as important as the final gathering on Easter Sunday. As I suspected a couple of days into the festivities,

Don Susano, my father-in-law, slaughtered the borrego on the beach in the early dawn and had it dressed out and ready for cooking before anyone had had their morning coffee.

For years, I thought of the borrego as being in the sheep family, primarily because of their taste and in spite of the fact that they have no wool. Spanish dictionaries made me doubt my choice and I never felt comfortable even after many inquiries to friends and family. Goat or sheep was the dilemma. I currently live with borregos as neighbors, or I should say neighbors raise borregos, and I enjoy their soft pleasant bleating at seven in the morning while they wait to be fed.

Decorated Pig's Head

Dance of the Pigs' Heads: 12 Diciembre

The Dance of the Pigs' Heads is performed and celebrated throughout the Yucatán peninsula, generally at the festival in which a town honors its patron saint. Though the Pig's Head ritual was considered pagan by the 16th century invaders, the Maya have managed to include the dance as a promesa, or sign of their faith in Christian festivals. The commitment to participate in this ceremony is a commitment for three years to life, not unlike the commitment of today's Maya to make a traditional pilgrimage to their village during its feria (fair).

The heads usually come from pigs raised by participants in their own yards, especially for this purpose. The pig is cooked slowly over hot coals in a pit. The body of the pig is cooked all day, wrapped in banana leaves and seasoned with achiote. The head is removed, placed on a tray, and decorated with flowers, paper ribbons, cutouts, miniature flags, fruit, and sometimes a bottle of liquor. In its mouth

Conmadre Perfidia dancing

Dance of the Pig's Head

is an ear of corn or piece of fruit. Each dancer holds a tray laden with a cooked and decorated pig's head on his or her own shiny, dark-haired head. Moving their feet in a pattern of slow, graceful circles on the stone floor, the dancers perform the jarana, or perhaps their own version of the "Dance of the Pigs' Heads." After a suitable length of time, a dancer passes his fifteen-pound tray on to the next who is worthy—or at least waiting eagerly—to balance the tray and dance.

At a pre-arranged hour, the dancers put down the trays and form a solemn procession, parading a banner depicting the patron saint around the church. They enter for a "*Nohoch Misa*" or High Mass.

Our town celebrates the twelfth of December, the Day of the Virgin of Guadalupe, along with the rest of the nation. Preparations begin on the fourth, which is Armando's *novena* (a Catholic devotion of prayer said typically on nine successive days). He is responsible for serving refreshments after the services on that day.

Quince Anos ceremony

The following eight nights, we gather at the church and receive the offerings of others. All of this culminates on the twelfth, when torch-carrying runners fulfill their promesa by running the 30 miles of unpaved road from Tulum to the lighthouse past Punta Allen. They generally arrive in time for the dance.

Mass is usually held by the visiting priest. If he cannot make it, the *monjas* from the *Convento* may assist the locals. If they cannot make it, we carry on by ourselves.

The chapel is brightly and lovingly adorned with a red, green and white banner with an image of the Virgin of Guadalupe superimposed on it. The crisp sounds of firecrackers signal the start of services; later, the same rapid-fire sound announces the close.

Those who stayed in the plaza to socialize or watch their children during the mass are now joined by the churchgoers. A live music group warms up for the hours of dancing that will continue until dawn. Most of the time I

Birthday girl's show

do not make it that long, much to Armando's disappointment. He seems to feel that we should dance every number even beyond my 3 a.m. point of exhaustion.

The free-to-all food—tacos of *pavo relleno* and cochinita pibil (the pig was not sacrificed in vain)—helps keep us going. The local cantina is usually closed for the day in order to open a "Superior Beer" stand at the fiesta. The first beer is usually on the house, in keeping with the tradition of fare for all.

Tizimin

Nestled in the northern Yucatán peninsula, within easy driving distance of Merida, Valladolid, and Cancún lies the garden of Tizimin. Here, vivid roses and heavily laden orange trees bend over ancient stone walls. In the heart of Maya cattle country, Tizimin numbers some 50,000 inhabitants: *charros* in boots and sombreros, stately ladies in traditional dress who search the market for the most tender cuts of beef, the reddest radishes, and the leafiest bouquets of lettuce. These are people who appreciate the nuances of tranquil living, but when it is time for a party then it's "*pura fiesta*."

Chichi—Grandmother

Until last year, every visit we made to Tizimin included a visit to Chichi, Armando's paternal grandmother. She sat in her mahogany rocker with her frail hands spread on the wide armrests and her eyes magnified through her glasses. Her vision was poor even with glasses, but that did not diminish her joy in our visit. As we chatted in the family way of easy small talk, catching up with news of relatives, Chichi liked to serve a small glass of whisky or rum. She was proud to be able to offer it, and prouder still to be in sufficiently good health to sip along with us. She always insisted on rising to slowly escort us to the door.

Mérida, Yucatán: Las Bombas (The Bombs or Jokes)

In Mérida on a hot afternoon, there are a multitude of restaurants and bars where you receive a different appetizer with each round of beer. The best known is La Prosperidad, which deserves a visit, preferably with a large group of friends.

Yucatecans know how to socialize. There is always much animated conversation and merriment on the small stage of La Prosperidad. Eventually, a beautiful mestiza in full huipil approaches the microphone and introduces herself and a companion. He is dressed in white shirt and pants with a red bandana and a hand-woven straw hat. They begin talking in a Maya-Spanish mix while they prepare *Las Bombas*. Their dialogue is quick and clever, sometimes making use of rhymes, double entendres, and puns, always ending in a punch line or "bomb." It is sort of like the old-time vaudeville routines in the U.S.—starting with, "Do you know what happened to me on the way to work?" "No, what?"

Mérida

Today we had breakfast with the "*Turkos*," the Lebanese of Mérida, downtown near the post office on the Alameda. There, elderly men play dice and sip strong coffee from little cups. Hot and delicious pita bread is eaten with skewered roasted lamb. A small plate of sour orange wedges, white onion and chile Habanero complete the condiments.

9

ROASTS AND RITUALS

La Corrida—Bullfight

The most famous fiesta in all Yucatán is the celebration of *Tres Reyes* in Tizimin. Days of festival culminate in a bullfight and communal feast. The modern bull replaces the deer once central to agricultural ritual. Overcoming the bull completes the cycle, and general feasting celebrates a year of prosperity.

Some scholars believe that the Yucatecan bullfight held during the celebration began before the Spanish arrived. They think it is related to an ancient ritual once performed on this same land. At that time, deer, which were plentiful, were pitted against men. Animal slaughter was part of the sacrificial rituals and contributed to feasting. Translating those traditions into today's festival, the bull is not wasted. Its death serves as part of the feast.

When I arrive in Tizimin for the celebration of Tres Reyes, there is a sense of festival in the air. The streets are crowded with visitors and residents alike. Local events

include displays of horsemanship, bullfights, rides, games of chance and booths selling baked goods, hand-embroidered dresses, and magic charms. The jewel in the crown of Tres Reyes is food.

Weeks of holiday feasting culminate in the banquet traditional for the day of January 6 itself: the Maya delicacy known as chocolomo. More than simply a meat dish, chocolomo is also an appreciation of the finest qualities of the prize animal from the bullfight. Succulent cuts of beef are presented with a piquant salsa of radishes and garnished with bright ribbons of lettuce, creating a repast both colorful and flavorful.

While savoring chocolomo, the Maya give thanks for the bounty of the old year and toast to good fortune in the new. The meal ends with a few sips of the fiery honey-based liqueur, *Xtabentun*, and a slice of *Rosca de Reyes*. Though this oval coffee bread is available from bakeries year round, on January 6th it is sold with a tiny baby doll baked inside. The person who discovers the doll is obliged to give yet another fiesta on February 2nd. The rosca, or crown, is decorated with candied fruit.

When I visit my extended family for Tres Reyes, one of our many activities is to go to the bullfight—*La Corrida*. Each year, the bullring is reconstructed in the style of the ancients, with poles and palm thatch to block the searing sun. Rustic ladders lead to the three stories that stand above the ground-level bullring.

The first time I carefully climbed the ladder-stairs, someone asked if I would like to sit on the

The Painted Fish and Other Mayan Feasts

veranda. I thought that sounded lovely, but I was shown to a plank on the edge of the ring that left my feet dangling just above the raging bull as he ran by.

As I later descended the shaky ladder, I could see the defeated bull being dressed directly outside the bullring on a cement platform. An adjoining butcher's table held scales and sharp knives used to prepare the kilos of meat for public sale. First, the eager buyers selected the appropriate accompaniments. In front of the butcher were long tables laden with attractively placed leafy lettuce, sprigs of cilantro, and bouquets of red radishes to complement the famous dish of chocolomo, freshly slaughtered bull.

I returned to my hosts' kitchen, confident that I was going to have the best chocolomo made that day. After all, I was to be inaugurated into this tradition in the home of the butcher. I stayed close by the cook, my sister-in-law, Chari. As she prepared large portions of the stock, I assisted by finely chopping the radishes.

It appeared that we were having guests. At that time, my Spanish was practically non-existent, so I was more comfortable chopping than talking. I did write down the day's events in my notebook— and of course, the recipe.

MEAT AND GAME

Chocolomo

Choco in Maya is hot, Lomo in Spanish is back. Chocolomo is a combination of Spanish and Maya, which evoke the origins of this festive dish. Traditionally, the meat for this variation of the universal boiled beef comes from the bull killed the same day at the corrida, or bullfight. Chocolomo is a favorite dish at celebrations throughout the Yucatán. It is a most unusual regional dish of liver, brains, kidney, heart, breast bones for their rich marrow, tail (if possible), and meat of a freshly slaughtered bull. The following version of the dish will probably be more appealing to most readers and their dining companions.

When visiting the States, I make this dish by simply substituting beef.

The meat is served on a platter, accompanied by Chiltomate salsa, ribbons of lettuce, and French bread. Salpicón salsa is added to the broth, which is served separately.

Ingredients:
4 lbs. beef with bone (chuck, round, brisket, skirt, or short ribs)
1 tbsp. salt
1 head garlic, flame roasted
3 cloves garlic, crushed
2 tsp. freshly ground black pepper
1 ½ tbsp. oregano, pan toasted
1 head butter lettuce, cross cut into ribbons
Chiltomate (see page 30)
Salpicón (see page 39)
Sweet French bread

Preparation:
Cut the meat into chunks and place in a large pot. Cover with water, add the salt and bring to a boil. Lower the heat to a simmer and skim off the grayish foam that forms on top. Continue simmering skimming for about 10 minutes. Add the garlic (roasted and fresh), the black pepper and the oregano. Cover and continue cooking until the meat is tender, about 2 hours. Remove the meat to a heated serving dish and keep hot. Skim as much of the fat as possible from the broth, then pour into a second pot through a double layer of cheesecloth or a fine mesh strainer. Heat the broth and ladle into bowls. Add Salpicón to taste to the broth. Place the lettuce ribbons in the bowl on top of the broth. Slice the meat and serve on a separate plate. The Chiltomate is eaten with the meat. Serves 6 to 8.

Pibil or Pit Cooking

Earthen pit cooking is a favorite way to prepare food for large crowds gathering for festivals and rituals. Digging the pit is easy at the beach in the sand. At the ranch the soil can be rocky so choosing the right place is important. Also, you do not want the cooking pit too far from the party as someone needs to check it from time to time. Usually the men cook the pib and exchange stories while watching the first flaming wood settle down into the hole to become coals. The next step is to place rocks on top of the coals to heat them. The container of seasoned uncooked food is placed on top of the rocks and covered with banana leaves followed by the soil. Cooking time depends on the volume and type of food, which most often is pig, turkey or deer.

Cochinita Pibil

Before the introduction of the domesticated pig, the Maya cooked wild boar in much the same way: marinated in achiote sauce, wrapped in banana leaves and buried in a pit with hot coals. It is one of the most famous local dishes. Mexican friends in Cancún prepare this on Sunday mornings for visitors. Although the dish is traditionally cooked in a pit, they use their kitchen oven or a clay pot on top of the stove to allow the juices to penetrate the meat. You can do the same. It's great for a party. Serve with tortillas for a rich brunch.

Ingredients:
    3 lbs. pork loin
    ½ cup bitter orange juice, or ⅓ cup
          orange juice and enough white
          vinegar to make ½ cup
    3 tbsp. recado rojo
    2 tbsp. recado for escabeche
    2 cloves garlic, crushed
    1 tsp. salt
    4 banana leaves (see below for directions
          to prepare)
    1 large red onion, diced
    ⅓ cup bitter orange juice, or ⅓ cup
          orange juice and white vinegar
          or lime juice to make ½ cup
    Salt to taste
    Ground chile Piquin
    2 Habanero chiles, minced

Preparation:
    Combine the bitter orange juice with the two recados, the garlic and the salt in a large bowl. Add the pork and mix to coat the pieces well. Cover loosely and set aside in the

refrigerator to marinate for 2 hours, stirring around from time to time.

Transfer the meat to a large flameproof casserole dish. Add 1 quart water, bring to a boil, lower the heat, top with 3 or 4 layers of banana leaves, cover and simmer for an hour and a half, or until tender. Check periodically, lifting up the leaves with care, to make sure there remains a small pool of sauce under the pork. Add water if necessary.

In the meantime, prepare a salsa by combining the onion, orange juice, and salt to taste.

When done place the pork on a heated platter. Pass the salsa, chile Piquin, and Habanero chiles separately. Serves 4 to 6.

To prepare fresh banana leaves:

Run each leaf over a medium flame on a stove or over a grill until it turns from shiny to opaque, turning so that both sides are treated. Cut down the middle with scissors to remove the spine. If using packaged leaves, run under very hot water to clean, then wipe dry with a cloth.

Carne Asada

Carne asada means roasted meat. Often this title means that the dish is going to be pork but it could be beef. So always, check for your preference when ordering in a restaurant.

Ingredients:
1 ½ lbs. flank or skirt steak, trimmed of any excess fat
2 tbsp. sour orange juice, or a mixture of orange and lime juice
1 tbsp. olive oil
Salt and freshly ground black pepper
½ tsp. each cumin and thyme (optional)
1 or 2 large cloves garlic, minced, according to taste
8 ½ inch thick slices of red onion
Additional olive oil
4 plantains
1 recipe Chiltomate Sauce

Preparation:
The meat should be about ½ inch thick. The skirt steak can be sliced horizontally, with the grain, to make 4 pieces. Mix the sour orange juice and the olive oil together and rub into the meat. Sprinkle with plenty of salt and pepper and the optional cumin and thyme. Distribute the garlic over the surface of the meat, pressing with the palms of your hands. Put on a plate and cover loosely with plastic wrap or invert another plate on top. Let stand at room temperature for 2 or 3 hours.

Prepare hot coals for grilling. With a wooden toothpick, poke a few holes in the peel of each plantain to allow steam to escape. Lay the plantains on the grill. Brush the onions with olive oil and put them on the grill next. Now add the steaks. The steaks should be cooked on the hottest part of the grill for 3 or 4 minutes on each side so that they are slightly charred on the outside and medium rare on the inside. When the meat is done, remove it to a cutting board and let it stand while the onions and plantains finish cooking. The onions and the plantains take about 10 minutes and should be turned frequently. Cut the meat diagonally across the grain and place in the center of a large heated platter. Arrange the grilled onions along one side. Slit the plantains lengthwise along one of the ridges and place on the other side of the carne asada.

Serve with Salsa Chiltomate. Serves 4.

Chuletas de Venado—Grilled Venison Chops

Yet another chance to use an achiote marinade.

Ingredients:

    4–6 venison chops, cut about 1 inch
        thick from the loin

    4 tbsp. recado rojo
    4 tbsp. orange juice
    4 tbsp. vinegar: sherry, red wine, or
        balsamic are all good
    4 tbsp. vegetable oil
    4 large cloves garlic minced
    ½ tsp. coarsely ground black pepper
    Salt to taste
    Salsa Chiltomate or Xnipek

Preparation:

Rinse the venison and pat dry with paper toweling. Trim off most of the rim fat from the chops. Put the recado rojo in a small bowl and add enough of the orange juice to make a paste; then add the rest of the juice, the vinegar, oil, garlic and pepper. Mix thoroughly and spread on the venison. Let the meat marinate, covered and in the refrigerator, for at least 12 hours and up to 2 days. Take the meat out when you start to fire up the grill. Cook the chops over medium hot coals on a lightly oiled grill until rare to medium rare, salting the meat as you turn it. This will take 6 to 8 minutes altogether, depending on the size of the chops. Serve with Salsa Chiltomate or Xnipek. Serves 4 to 6.

Grilled Lamb Marinated in Sour Orange

Unless you happen to have a spit, this is an easier way to grill a leg of lamb.

Ingredients:

        1 butterflied leg of lamb (4 to 5 lbs.),
                your butcher will do this for you
        1 tbsp. ground cumin
        1 tbsp. black pepper
        1 tbsp. thyme
        2 tbsp. oregano
        ½ cup sour orange juice or 6 tbsp.
                orange juice and 2 tbsp. lime
                juice
        3 tbsp. olive oil
        ½ tsp. salt

Preparation:

Toast the spices in a small skillet over medium heat, stirring often, until the mixture smells roasted, taking care not to scorch it. Combine the spices with the sour orange juice, olive oil and salt. Rub the mixture all over the lamb and let it marinate in the refrigerator for at least 6 hours, or overnight. Take the lamb from the refrigerator several hours before grilling. Prepare hot coals. Grill the lamb 4 inches above the hot coals, basting with any remaining marinade, about 20 minutes on each side for medium rare. Check after half an hour. When done, remove it from the grill and let it sit for 10 minutes before cutting into thin slices.

Serve with Salsa Chiltomate or Mango Salsa with Spearmint. Serves 8.

Picadillo

This is especially good as a stuffing for chile relleno, empanadas, squash or as a filling for a soft taco lunch.

Ingredients:

        2 tbsp. oil
        1 lb. lean ground beef
        1 cup chopped onion
        1 large clove garlic, minced
        1 cup peeled, seeded and chopped plum
                tomato
        ¼ tsp. each cumin, cinnamon, allspice
                and cloves
        Salt and pepper to taste
        ¼ cup small Spanish olives, quartered
        ¼ cup raisins

Preparation:

Heat the oil in a large, heavy skillet. Brown the meat, breaking it apart with a fork as it cooks. Add the onions and garlic and cook until tender. Add the remaining ingredients and simmer, uncovered, for about 20 minutes. Makes about 1 quart

Note: Part or all lean ground pork can be used to good effect, or substitute ground turkey if you like.

Poc Chuc

You may make Poc Chuc, which refers to marinade and grilling, with beef, pork or venison. The important thing to include is the Salsa Chiltomate and marinated onion.

Ingredients:

4 loin pork chops, about 1 inch thick
½ cup sour orange juice or 6 tbsp. orange
    juice and 2 tbsp. lime juice
2 large cloves garlic, minced
½ tsp. salt
1 tsp. freshly ground pepper
Salsa Chiltomate
Cebollas Encurtidas

Preparation:

Combine the sour orange juice, garlic, salt and pepper. Rub the mixture onto the pork chops and let marinate for 2 hours turning from time to time.

Cook the chops over medium coals on a lightly oiled grill, basting frequently, until done—about 20 minutes. Serve with Salsa Chiltomate and Cebollas Encurtidas. Serves 4.

Puchero de Tres Carnes—Three Meat Stew

It is still the custom in many homes in Campeche to serve *Puchero* every Monday. Here is a version to try in your own kitchen.

Ingredients:

1 lb. pork shoulder, cubed
1 lb. beef chuck, cubed
4 whole chicken thighs
1 lb. marrow bones (optional)
1 stick cinnamon
8 whole black peppercorns
Salt to taste
1 tsp. saffron threads
1 head garlic
2 onions, diced
2 large carrots, halved lengthwise and
    cut into 1-inch pieces
2 sweet potatoes cut into 1-inch chunks
2 chayote cut lengthwise into quarters
2 platanos (cooking bananas) cut
    crosswise into 1-inch pieces

½ cabbage, cut into small wedges
2 ears of corn cut crosswise into 1-inch
  pieces
2 cups cooked garbanzo beans
2 tbsp. chopped mint
4 tbsp. chopped cilantro
Arroz Blanco
Salsa Tamulada
Salpicón
2 firm, ripe avocados cut in ½-inch
  cubes

Preparation:

Place the chicken, pork, beef and optional bones in a large pot and cover with cold water. Bring to a boil, skim and season with salt, pepper, cinnamon, saffron, garlic and onions. Lower the heat, cover and simmer for an hour. Add the vegetables and the garbanzo beans and cook for half an hour or until the meats and vegetables are tender. Take out the chicken and set aside to cool a bit. Take out the vegetables with a slotted spoon and put them in a large deep platter. Remove the chicken meat from the bone in large pieces and arrange all the meats on the vegetables. Skim the fat from the broth, and strain some of it over the platter, pouring any extra into a bowl to pass separately. Garnish the Puchero with chopped cilantro and mint. Accompany the dish with Arroz Blanco, Salpicón, Salsa Tamulada and avocado in separate dishes. Serves 6 to 8.

Conejo Estilo de Merida—Braised Rabbit Merida Style

This is a rich, sweet, sumptuous taste you will want to repeat.

Ingredients:

1 rabbit, cut up
Salt and pepper
2 tbsp. olive oil
¼ cup brandy
1 large white onion, halved lengthwise
  and cut into slivers
2 sweet red peppers, charred, peeled,
  seeded, and cut into strips
½ tsp. thyme
1 tsp. marjoram
1 cup chicken broth
½ cup dry sherry
12 small pitted prunes
½ cup sour cream

Preparation:

Rinse the rabbit pieces and pat dry with paper toweling. Sprinkle with salt and pepper.

Heat the oil in a large frying pan. Add the rabbit and sauté until golden brown. Pour in the brandy and flame it. Add the onion to the pan, cover and cook over low heat for 15 minutes. Add the red peppers, thyme, marjoram, chicken broth sherry and prunes and cook for 45 minutes. Take out the rabbit pieces and put onto a heated platter. Stir the sour cream into the sauce, heat to a simmer and spoon over the rabbit. Serves 4.

Venado Guisado—Braised Venison

Venison is often helped by marinating and slow cooking as in this dish.

Ingredients:

2–3 lbs. venison from the loin or leg
4 tbsp. recado rojo
¼ cup orange juice
¼ cup vinegar (sherry, red wine or balsamic)
¼ cup vegetable oil
4 large cloves garlic, minced
½ tsp. salt, plus additional salt to taste
½ tsp. coarsely ground pepper
2 cups beef broth
2 tbsp. olive oil
1 large white onion, chopped
4 ounces smoked ham, slivered
1 lb. plum tomatoes, seeded and chopped
1 bay leaf
1 tbsp. fresh oregano or 1 teaspoon dried
2 tbsp. fresh mint, chopped

Preparation:

Trim off the fat from the venison before cutting into 1-inch cubes. Put the recado into a glass or stainless steel bowl large enough to hold the meat easily. Add some of the orange juice to the recado to make a smooth paste; then stir in the rest of the juice, the vinegar, oil, garlic, ½ teaspoon salt, and the pepper. Add the cubed venison and stir to coat. Let the meat stand, covered, in the refrigerator for at least 12 hours or up to 2 days, stirring from time to time. Remove the venison from the refrigerator an hour or so before making the dish so that the meat will come up to room temperature (this helps ensure that the cooked venison will be moist). Heat the oil in a deep skillet over a medium flame. Add the onion and cook, stirring, until soft. Add the slivered ham and the chopped tomato. Sauté for a couple of minutes and then raise the heat to let the accumulated juices boil away. Transfer the venison from the bowl to the pan using a slotted spoon. Stir and cook, still over high heat, for 5 minutes. Add the broth, bay leaf, oregano and any remaining marinade. Bring to a boil, lower the heat, cover and let simmer for half an hour. Taste for salt and stir in the mint.

Serve with rice or flat noodles as in stroganoff. Serves 6 to 8.

Dzik de Venado—Shredded Deer

Well-cooked venison torn into shreds, then marinated in a salpicón, and served with warm tortillas or tostaditas. A good party item.

Ingredients:
> 1 ½ pounds venison from the loin or
>   sirloin
> 2 tbsp. vegetable oil
> 1 tsp. salt
> 1 tsp. coarsely ground black pepper
> Salpicón
> 1 cup finely chopped radishes
> 4 Serrano chiles, minced
> 1 sweet green pepper, finely chopped
> 1 medium white onion, finely chopped
> ½ tsp. salt
> ½ cup bitter orange juice, or ⅓ cup
>   orange juice and enough lime
>   juice or white vinegar to make
>   ½ cup

Preparation:
Trim any fat and gristle from the meat. Cut into 1-inch thick steaks along the grain, (not against it or the meat will not pull apart property), rub with oil, salt and pepper, and cut into 2-inch pieces. Put in a large shallow pan, add enough water to barely cover, bring to a boil and simmer for 45 minutes. Let the meat cool in the broth. Remove the venison from the broth and shred roughly. Combine the ingredients for the salpicón, combine with the venison and let stand for an hour. Serve at room temperature. Serves 6.

Langoniza de Valladolid—Venison Sausage

Originally from the colonial Yucatecan town of Valladolid about ten minutes from the Chichén Itzá ruins, this sausage is often served in scrambled eggs.

Ingredients:
> 1 ½ lb. venison shoulder, trimmed of
>   all fat
> 1 lb. boneless pork, any gristle removed
> ½ lb. pork back fat
> ½ lb. slab bacon, rind removed
> ½ cup recado rojo

3 large cloves garlic, chopped
1 large red onion, chopped
4 tsp. sea salt
1 tbsp. coarsely ground black pepper
2 tbsp. dried oregano
½ tsp. ground cloves
1 tsp. ground allspice
1 cup vinegar: sherry, red wine or
      balsamic
Medium sized pork casings (optional)

Preparation:

Cut the meats and fat into thin 2-inch strips and place in a glass, enamel or stainless steel bowl. Put the onion, garlic, recado, and spices into a blender jar and blend until smooth. Pour the mixture over the meats and stir thoroughly. Cover and put in the refrigerator to marinate for 12 to 18 hours, stirring a few times during the process. Then, grind the mixture through a ¼-inch plate. Knead thoroughly, blending in any juices remaining in the bowl. Stuff into pork casings and tie into 6-inch lengths. Dry the sausage overnight before cooking. Use within a couple of days or freeze them. You can also divide the bulk sausage to use as patties for a breakfast buffet or as *chorizo* in chili con carne. If you have a smoker, you can smoke them as the Maya traditionally do. These will keep 3 days refrigerated, 2 months frozen. Makes about 4 pounds.

Fair grounds in Tizimin

10

GIFTS FROM THE BEE GOD: DESSERTS AND OTHER SWEETS

Honey

Aromatic honey of the region, fermented with bark of the balche tree, was the ritual drink of the Maya jaguar priests. Today the fiery liqueur, Xtabentun, derives its name and flavor from local honey. Important trade items in the past, honey and cacao now delight the palate in desserts and drinks. *Buñuelos* (fried pastries dipped in honey), *caballeros pobres* (a regional bread pudding), and *flan*, as well as fresh fruit desserts and other treats, appear in this chapter.

Ancient stories and glyphs tell about bee keeping among the Maya. It is still respected work in the jungle. The natural powers of royal jelly and honey make the Yucatán peninsula a major market for the products of bees. Today's bees that make "jungle honey," as I call it, have crossed with Killer African Bees that passed through our area several years ago.

After the arrival of the Killer African Bees, my neighbor Lela and her sister Juana were clearing some of their property

along the coast. They made quite a disturbance chopping and cutting the lot, so a swarm of annoyed Africans chased Juana. She finally dropped to the ground in hopes that the swarm would pass above her, which it did. However, Lela counted 34 stingers that she extracted from her sister's sleeveless arms and even from her upper torso, which had been covered by her blouse. Juana is a strong woman and dealt with the pain without complaining. While the bees are dangerous, this new honey has a wonderful flavor and is good for you.

Though Maya meals rarely include dessert, people of the peninsula eat desserts any time of day. The following recipes are carefully developed cakes and cookies designed to please the American palate and use familiar baking techniques. My long time friend and sometimes sidekick Donna Nielson has been a wizard at converting the subtleties of Yucatec dishes for this book but she really shines in the dessert department, as will be seen as you work your way through this section.

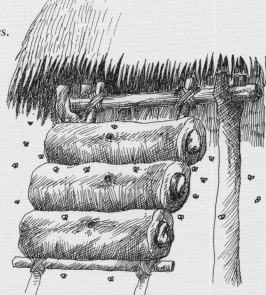

The Painted Fish and Other Mayan Feasts

Budin de Pan—Bread Pudding

A universal technique to transform day-old bread is included here. In Mexico, *pan dulces* or sweet breads are readily available to substitute for the French bread eliminating the need for sugar and honey.

Mix in a 9 inch x 13 inch glass or ceramic baking pan:

    4 cups coarsely crumbled, day-old, sweet French bread, crusts removed
    ½ cup raisins

Beat well together:

    3 large eggs
    3 cups whole milk
    ½ tsp. salt
    ½ tsp. cinnamon
    Juice and zest of 1 lime
    2 tsp. vanilla extract or 2 tbsp. dark rum
    3 tbsp. honey
    2 tbsp. sugar

Preparation:

Pour this mixture over the bread crumbs. Let stand 15 minutes and then bake in a moderate oven for about 35 minutes, or until set. Serve warm or cold with a dab of pineapple marmalade or other preserve on top.

Crema Inglesa—Cream Sauce

Ingredients:

    2 cups milk
    ⅔ cup sugar
    6 large egg yolks
    1 stick whole cinnamon
    1 tsp. pure vanilla extract

Preparation:

Heat the milk with the cinnamon stick until hot and let stand half an hour. Mix the sugar and the egg yolks in a bowl. Remove the cinnamon stick from the pan and reheat the milk until very hot. Ladle about ½ cup into the egg mixture, whisking rapidly. Return this mixture to the rest of the milk and stir constantly over medium low heat until it thickens and just coats the spoon—about 7 to 10 minutes. Pour into a bowl through a fine mesh strainer. Cool and then chill. Makes 3 cups.

Orange Crema Inglesa

Instead of the cinnamon stick, heat the milk with the peel of 2 oranges. This sauce is good with chocolate desserts and with plain fruit—mango and banana—as a dessert.

Crepas Estilo de Maya—Mayan crepes

This is a spectacular dessert! The sight of the flames cascading down the swirl of orange peel to ignite the pan is breathtaking. Time consuming but not very difficult at all, much of the recipe can be prepared ahead of time. You can make the crepes a day or two ahead, fill them in the afternoon and then flame them just before serving. Do a trial run-through for your family or friends—they will be entertained!

Crepas
Ingredients:
> 1 cup milk
> ½ cup water
> 3 egg yolks
> 1 ½ cups sifted flour
> 3 tbsp. brandy
> 5 tbsp. melted butter

Preparation:

Measure the ingredients in order into a blender. Process for a minute, scrape down the sides with a rubber spatula and process a few seconds longer. Pour into a small bowl, cover, and refrigerate overnight.

To cook the crepas, you will need a sauté pan 5 or 6 inches in diameter, a small ladle, a few tablespoons of vegetable oil in a cup, and a brush.

Brush the pan with oil and heat over a medium hot flame until a drop of water sizzles in it. Lift the pan from the flame and pour in about 3 tbsp. of the batter, tilting the pan so that the entire surface is covered. Add a few drops of batter if necessary or pour back any excess into the bowl. Put the pan back on the flame and cook the crepa for about a minute, or until light brown. Lift the edge up with a spatula and flip the crepa over with your fingertips. Let it cook another half minute and turn out onto a plate. Brush the pan with a bit more oil and repeat the process until all the crepas are cooked.

If you are making crepes ahead, wrap them well in plastic or cover them with another plate and keep in the refrigerator until you are ready to use them. Makes 12.

Assembling the crepas:
> 3 bananas, thinly sliced
> 3 tbsp. sugar
> 3 tbsp. dark rum
> 1 large whole orange
> 3 tbsp. butter
> ½ cup sugar
> ½ cup brandy
> ¼ cup orange liqueur

Sprinkle the sugar and rum over the bananas in a bowl, mix gently, and let stand for half an hour. Mix again and fill each crepa, leaving the best-looking side out, roll it up, and set aside on a plate.

For the flambé event, you will need a chafing dish, a spatula, a cooking spoon, and a small, long handled heatproof pitcher, or a ladle.

Cut the orange peel in a thin spiral, leaving it attached at the stem end. Heat the chafing dish. Add the butter and the ½-cup sugar and heat until it is bubbling. Carefully place the filled crepas in the pan, seam side down. Cook for a couple of minutes and then turn carefully. Warm the brandy in the pitcher or the ladle—don't let it boil or it won't fire. Pour the orange liqueur over the crepas. Impale the orange on a knife blade and hold the orange aloft over the chafing dish with the tip end of the peel just touching the syrup. Have someone ignite the brandy for you and then pour it onto the peel from near the stem end. The flame will travel the length of the peel and the entire chafing dish will ignite spectacularly. Spoon the flaming liqueur over the crepas until the fire is out and serve. Serves 6.

Note: If you are going to try this on your stove, be sure to turn off the fan when you start the flames going.

Note: The crepas can also be filled with strawberry or pineapple preserves flavored with a little rum.

Cuzan Tropical Cheese Tart

Ingredients:
1 ¼ cups graham cracker crumbs
⅓ cup sugar
¼ lb. butter, melted
½ tsp. cinnamon
12 oz. cream cheese
2 eggs, lightly beaten
½ cup sugar
1 tbsp. rum
1 tbsp. orange liqueur
1 tsp. lime juice
1 tsp. lime zest
1 cup sour cream
3 tbsp. sugar
1 tbsp. rum

All ingredients should be room temperature.

Preparation:
Preheat the oven to 375 degrees.
In a small bowl mix together the crumbs, sugar, cinnamon and butter. Press into a 9-inch pie plate and bake for 10 minutes.

Whip the cream cheese until fluffy. Add the sugar, eggs, rum, orange liqueur, lime zest, juice, and mix until smooth. Pour into the pie shell and bake for 20 minutes.

Mix the sour cream, sugar and rum. Spread carefully on top and return to the oven for 5 minutes. Let cool on a rack and then refrigerate for several hours before serving.

Dulce de Papaya—Papaya Sweet

This is a traditional dish and I have seen vats of it made at once since it keeps well due to all the sugar.

Ingredients:
> 2 green, unripe papayas, peeled, cut in half lengthwise and seeded
> 1 cup sugar
> 3 cups water
> 2 cinnamon sticks, each about 2 inches long
> Vanilla ice cream

Preparation:
Put the sugar, water and cinnamon into a pan just wide enough to hold the papaya halves in one layer. Bring to a boil, stirring occasionally. Add the papaya halves and cook, uncovered, at a low boil for about 1 ¼ hours, turning occasionally. The papaya will be translucent and the liquid thickened into syrup. Remove from the heat, discard the cinnamon and let cool.

Divide the papaya halves between 4 bowls. Spoon some of the syrup around them and put a scoop of vanilla ice cream in the center. Serves 4.

Variation: Dulce de Mango Verde—Green Mango Sweet

Substitute 3 or 4 green, unripe mangoes for the papayas. Peel them and cut into even pieces while avoiding the stringiness of the flesh near the pit.

Prepare in the same way as Dulce de Papaya. Spoon into bowls and top with vanilla ice cream or creme fraiche.

Flan

Flan, or egg custard, has Spanish roots but the French also have a creme caramel that resembles this fine dessert or nutritious snack. It is popular throughout Mexico with many variations like the two mentioned here that will be a hit with your audience.

Ingredients:

- 2 cups milk
- 2 cups half-and-half (or 3 cups milk and
    1 cup heavy cream)
- 1 stick cinnamon
- 1 vanilla bean split lengthwise
- ⅔ cup sugar
- 6 eggs
- 4 egg yolks
- 1 cup sugar
- 3 tbsp. water

Preparation:

Preheat the oven to 350 degrees.

Put the milk and cream into a heavy saucepan. Add the split vanilla bean, scraping out the inside contents with the tip of a small sharp knife, and the cinnamon stick. Set aside.

In a saucepan mix the 1 cup sugar and 3 tablespoons water and bring to a boil, stirring. Continue cooking until the sugar is colored a deep amber. Pour the caramel around the bottom and sides of a warm 2-quart baking dish or individual custard cups.

Whisk together the eggs, egg yolks and ⅔ cup sugar. Remove the vanilla bean and the cinnamon stick from the milk mixture and combine with the beaten eggs. Set the baking dish or baking cups in a pan of hot water. Strain the custard mixture into a bowl or a large pitcher and pour into the baking cups.

Bake for 25 minutes to an hour, depending on the pan, until a knife inserted in the center comes out clean. Cool on a rack and chill thoroughly. To serve, unmold onto a platter or individual serving dishes. Serves 6 to 8.

Note: vanilla extract can be used instead of the vanilla bean—add it to the custard mixture just before baking.

Kahlua Flan

Leave out the vanilla and cinnamon and add 2 tbsp. Kahlua to the strained custard mixture.

Tasty flan

Flan with Glazed Mango

Ingredients:

    2 cups milk
    2 cups half-and-half (or 3 cups milk and
        1 cup heavy cream)
    1 stick cinnamon
    ⅔ cup sugar
    6 eggs
    4 egg yolks
    1 tsp. vanilla
    1 tbsp. dark rum
    1 cup sugar
    3 tbsp. water
    Glazed mango garnish (see below)

Preparation:

Preheat the oven to 350 degrees.

Bring the milk and cream just to a boil with the cinnamon stick. Let stand while whisking together the eggs, egg yolks and ⅔ cup sugar. Take out the cinnamon stick and combine the two mixtures. Add the vanilla and rum and set aside.

In a saucepan mix the 1 cup sugar and 3 tablespoons water and bring to a boil, stirring. Continue cooking until the sugar is colored a deep amber. Pour the caramel around the bottom and sides of a warm 2-quart baking dish. Pour in the custard mixture through a strainer and set the dish in a pan of hot water.

Bake for 45 minutes to an hour, until a knife inserted in the center comes out clean. Cool on a rack and chill thoroughly. To serve, unmold on a platter and spoon glazed mango around the edge. Serves 6 to 8.

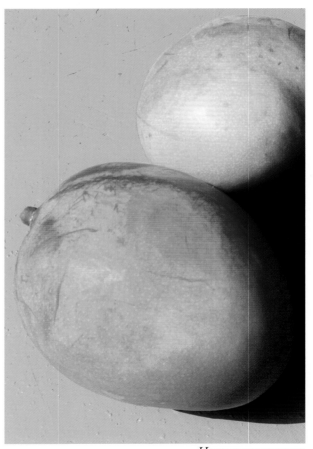

Home grown mangoes

Glazed Mango

Ingredients:

    2 firm ripe mangoes
    1 cup sugar
    1 cup water
    1 inch piece of lemon zest

Preparation:

    In a saucepan, combine the water and sugar and bring to a boil. Add the lemon zest and cook for 5 minutes. Peel the mangoes. To slice, place each one stem side down on a cutting surface, narrow side toward you. Cut through on both sides of the seed. Slice or cube the pieces. Add to the syrup, cover and simmer for 1 minute. Let cool in the syrup and chill.

Galletas de Lima—Lime Cookies

Ingredients:

    ½ cup softened butter
    ⅔ cup sugar
    1 tsp. vanilla
    1 slightly beaten egg
    2 tbsp. lime juice
    1 tsp. finely grated lime zest
    1 ½ cups flour

    1 ½ tsp. baking powder
    ¼ tsp. salt
    2 tbsp. softened butter
    ¼ cup sugar

Preparation:

    Preheat the oven to 350 degrees. Cream the butter and sugar. Add the vanilla, egg, lime juice and lime zest. Blend well. Sift together the flour, baking powder and salt. Add this mixture gradually to the cookie batter and beat until glossy, about 3 minutes. Cover the dough with plastic and refrigerate for half an hour. Form teaspoonfuls of the dough into balls and place on ungreased cookie sheets 2 ½ inches apart and 1 ½ inches from the sides of the pans. Put the 2 tablespoons butter and the ¼ cup sugar on two small flat plates. Take a 2-inch, flat-bottomed glass and rub the bottom in the butter to grease it, then dip it in the sugar and stamp each ball of dough flat. Dip the glass bottom in the butter and sugar frequently to avoid sticking. Bake about 10 minutes, or until the edges of the cookies are golden brown. Remove them from the cookie sheets immediately and cool on a wire rack. Makes 3 dozen 2-inch cookies.

Orange Oatmeal Cookies

Ingredients:

¾ cup butter
1 ½ cups sugar
2 eggs
1 tsp. vanilla
4 tbsp. grated orange peel
¼ cup milk
2 cups flour
½ tsp. salt
1 tsp. soda
1 ½ cups raisins
3 cups rolled oats
1 cup moist shredded coconut

Preparation:

Beat together the butter and sugar in a large bowl. Add the eggs, vanilla, orange peel and milk. Combine the flour, salt and soda and gradually stir into the butter mixture. Stir in the raisins, rolled oats and coconut. Blend well. Drop by level teaspoons onto lightly oiled cookie sheets, placing dough about 2 inches apart. Bake in a moderate oven for 10 minutes, or until the edges are golden brown. Let the cookies cool on the pan for about a minute, then transfer them to wire racks to cool completely. Makes about 6 dozen.

Cuzan Chocolate Cake

Ingredients:

½ cup butter
⅔ cup sugar
1 egg
1 tbsp. orange liqueur
⅓ cup sugar
⅓ cup unsweetened cocoa
1 tsp. cinnamon
1 tsp. instant espresso coffee powder
  (optional)
½ tsp. salt
1 tsp. soda
1 ¼ cups sifted all purpose flour
¾ cup plain yogurt

Preparation:

Preheat the oven to 350 degrees. Cream together the butter and ⅔ cup sugar. Beat in the egg and orange liqueur.

Sift together the ⅓ cup sugar, cocoa, cinnamon, coffee powder, salt and soda and stir into the butter mixture. Add the flour in two parts alternately with the yogurt. Beat the batter just until smooth after each addition. Pour the batter into a greased 9-inch square pan and bake for 45 minutes. We serve this cake with whipped, sweetened creme fraiche. Ice cream or regular whipped cream is also good.

Banana Cake

Ingredients:

    2 cups flour
    1 tsp. baking soda
    1 tsp. cinnamon
    ¼ tsp. baking powder
    ¼ tsp. salt
    1 tbsp. grated orange peel
    ⅔ cup butter
    1 ¼ cups sugar
    2 large eggs
    1 cup mashed ripe banana
    2 tbsp. yogurt
    2 tsp. vanilla extract
    ½ cup floured raisins

Preparation:

Sift the first six ingredients into a medium bowl. Cream together the butter and sugar in a large bowl. Add the eggs, one at a time, then the orange peel. Mix the yogurt together with the mashed banana. Add half the flour mixture to the bowl and mix. Mix in the banana mixture and then the rest of the flour. Add the vanilla and stir until thoroughly combined. Fold in the raisins. Pour into a greased and floured 9-inch square pan and bake for about 40 minutes in a moderate oven. Let cool and then remove from the pan. Serves 12.

Pastel de Zanahoria—Carrot Cake

Ingredients:

    ¾ cup softened butter
    1 cup sugar (turbinado sugar works very
        well here)
    2 eggs
    1 ½ tsp. vanilla
    1 tbsp. grated orange zest
    1 cup packed, finely grated carrot
    2 cups unbleached, all-purpose flour
    ½ tsp. salt
    ¼ tsp. baking soda
    1 ½ tsp. baking powder
    ¼ cup orange juice
    ½ cup milk
    Lime Glaze (optional: see below)

Preparation:

Preheat the oven to 350 degrees. Butter and flour an 8-inch square pan. Cream together the butter and sugar. Add the eggs, one at a time, mixing to blend after each addition. Add the vanilla, orange zest and grated carrot. Sift together the flour, salt, soda and baking powder. Add half the flour mixture to the batter and mix. Add the orange juice and milk together, and then the remainder of the flour mixture, beating well after each addition. Spread evenly in the prepared pan and bake for about 40 minutes, or until a toothpick inserted in the center comes out clean. Let stand for 10 minutes before turning out onto a wire rack to cool completely. Brush the top with the Lime Glaze if you like, and/or serve with whipped cream or vanilla ice cream.

Lime Glaze

In a small bowl put ⅔ cup sifted confectioners' sugar. Add 2 tbsp. lime juice and mix until smooth.

Budin de Arroz—Rice Pudding

Ingredients:
    1 cup short grain rice
    ¼ tsp. salt
    2 cups water
    1 ⅔ cups sugar
    Zest of an orange or a large limón
    6 cups hot milk
    ½ to 1 cup raisins
    3 egg yolks, well beaten
    2 tsp. vanilla extract or 2 tbsp. añejo rum
    Cinnamon

Preparation:
    Soak the rice in enough hot water to cover for 15 minutes. Drain, rinse in cold water and drain again. Place in a saucepan; add the salt and 2 cups of water. Bring to a boil, reduce the heat, cover and cook over very low heat until the water has been absorbed. Let stand a few minutes off the heat. Fluff with a fork and slowly add the milk, stirring well to avoid lumping. Add the sugar, the zest, and the raisins and cook over low heat, stirring often, until the milk has been absorbed. Stir in the egg yolks and the vanilla or the añejo. Cook a few minutes longer and turn into a serving bowl or individual dishes. Sprinkle lightly with cinnamon. Serves 8 to 12.

THIRST QUENCHERS

Michelada

This drink is a great hangover cure, or nice and refreshing on a hot afternoon while you prepare a ceviche.

Salt the rim of a tall glass, add: ice, a shot of fresh squeezed lime juice, dash of Maggi Sauce/soy sauce, half a shot of Worchestershire sauce, dash or 2 of Tabasco depending on your tolerance for spice, and pour in your favorite Mexican beer.

Variation: add 2 shots of Clamato (tomato juice with clam juice) and some black pepper to taste.

Cuzan Margarita

Mojito

Always refreshing but dangerously delicious!
> In a highball glass crush together:
> 5 leaves of mint,
> 2 fine sliced lime circles, and
> 2 tablespoons of turbinado sugar (or use light brown sugar),
> add ice, pour in a shot of your favorite white rum, and a dash of carbonated water.
> Garnish glass with a lime circle and enjoy!

Tequila Punch

> Ice:
> 1 qt. fresh squeezed grapefruit juice (or your favorite refrigerated juice, ex: Tropicana)
> 1 qt. fresh squeezed orange juice (or your favorite refrigerated juice)
> 1 qt. Tequila
> 1 pint orange liqueur
> ⅓–½ cup grenadine, for some color and sweetener. Add ⅓ cup and taste, if it's not sweet enough, add more grenadine.
> Thin sliced orange and lime circles to float on top
> Mix all liquids in your favorite punch bowl, add ice and float fruit slices on top.

Margarita

This is the easiest recipe, really! It always gets the most compliments! Don't you dare use a sour mix! It contains only 3 ingredients and should never be blended or frozen! You don't even need to use a fancy or expensive tequila!
> Salt the rim of your favorite margarita glass
> One shot fresh squeezed lime juice (this is the key, no extra sweeteners!)
> One shot orange liqueur
> One shot of your favorite tequila
> Pour these 3 ingredients over ice in a shaker, shake well, serve in salted glass, and enjoy! Your guests will be very impressed!

EPILOGUE

I remember the sunshiny day Glenn Cowles and his family first visited Punta Allen. They were adventurous travelers but there was another reason that Glenn ventured into Cuzan Guest House. He quite bluntly but softly drawled, "Sonja, you know you have bonefish here." A flash of understanding jolted my body. Having caught my first bonefish in the Grand Cayman islands fifteen years before, I had an idea of the impact flyfishing could have on our business. Always the skeptic, I suggested we see for ourselves and prepared to explore in our twenty-five foot launcha. Glenn gathered his gear and we climbed into the boat from thigh deep, clear water. Hauling the anchor, Armando gave me a quizzical look, but always ready for a sea voyage, he took charge and soon we skimmed across what resembled a flat azure lake. Armando slowed as we entered a cove and we immediately noticed nervous water. It was obvious that something was going on just below the surface. Glenn cast into the large ripples and wham, his line tightened and he began reeling and releasing, reeling and releasing, bringing in the fish. It was a bonefish! However, it was snagged on its side and not taking a fly caught in its mouth. The surrounding fish seemed to be mostly happy mullet. Glenn, a true flyfisherman looked slightly sheepish and rejected this as proof of his hypotheses that we had an abundance of "bones" and a new direction for our business. I, however, saw in this small display of flyfishing great possibilities and immediately shifted my business paradigm to saltwater flyfishing for bonefish, tarpon and permit.

Those days there were no fishing rods of any kind in the village. Locals used spear guns, gaffs, hand lines and nets for fishing. Slowly, I began to explain flyfishing to our lobster-fishermen-turned-nature-guides. At first, they refused to handle a rod. They resisted learning to toss a line back and forth with finesse to make a "presentation" to the fish they had spotted without "spooking" it. This they initially left up to the clients. They were excellent at spotting fish for the client and learned to maneuver the large boat without getting too close or making too much noise, and felt that was their job. The guides embraced the work and with their thorough knowledge of Ascension Bay, our new direction into the world of flyfishing began. We have Glenn to thank for it. He continued to visit us with avid angler friends we labeled as the "Memphis connection." Many others along the way helped give confidence to our guides in their ability to master "fishing English." Later, with the second generation of guides, their English became proficient along with their casting skills.

The flyfishing market felt like a gift. In addition to the university milieu, I was surrounded by intelligent (flyfishing has been described as the thinking man's sport), conservation minded and accomplished men and women. That suited me just fine. When people inevitably asked if I fished, my reply was I "had" fished and now I just liked to hang out with fishermen. I was a facilitator for boats, guides, food, rooms and a steady stream of what I called "normal people"or non-angler types that sought comfort in our rustic setting and stayed a few days to enjoy snorkeling,

birding and hammock time. In the evening, guests gathered for fresh lime margaritas followed by a seafood dinner in the breezy, sand-floor palapa dining room.

Each new group of fly fishermen taught me and our guides something and the guides showed the guests their backyard: the magnificent, gin-clear flats of Ascension Bay. Being the first to bring tourism to the village, Armando and I felt a huge responsibility to bring prosperity and right livilihood to our neighbors and ourselves. The establishment of the world biosphere reserve aided in these endeavors and more fishing lodges opened and shared the rich waters. Sun resistant fabric shirts and hats with polarized sunglasses gradually became the uniform of the guides. Our guides have always been from Punta Allen, born and bred, sons of the first guides we trained. The new generations are proud of their casting skills as well as their guiding skills and ability to communicate in English.

I hosted intrepid anglers from many corners of the world as Armando staunchly decided not to learn English. I felt he was somewhat justified as he already spoke two languages: Maya and Spanish. I loved my role, as I was eager to speak English and hear about what was going on in the world. We still had no electricity but had rudimentary lighting from a solar-powered electrical system we had installed. Any news came from the battery operated radio in Spanish and an occasional newspaper or magazine brought by visitors. The isolation agreed with me for a while but I was beginning to wonder if I should be more connected to the outside world.

More organization and more business meant more trips to Cancún for mail and supplies. Playa del Carmen was just beginning to grow and had no phones or post office. When the fax machine became a popular means of communication, I preferred to go to the magical island of Cozumel on the ferry, an agreeable boat ride from Playa, to seek any communication I might have waiting for me. The entire coast was yet to be connected to the ethers so I sought out a friendly real estate office willing to receive and send my infrequent faxes. I traveled there weekly, picked up any business inquiries and went next door to the La Choza restaurant. The staff

began to recognize me as I ordered a fine lunch and sat back to read faxes and respond to our early customers.

Later, we turned south to Felipe Carrillo Puerto for shopping and communication as Tulum remained a sleepy town without services. In Carrillo, as we call it for short, we found another community of friends and a structure to work with: electricity, phones and a telegraph office. We stayed in one of the two hotels: the Faisan and Venado or the Hotel Esquivel on our shopping excursions. Later, a friend rented us one room made of block with a tin roof where we stored a hammock to sleep in while there. Still later, a friend was moving back to his home in Chetumal and we bought his unfinished house and gradually created living and office space, as well as room for frequent visits of family and friends.

These changes brought increased staff and a need for me to be less hands-on in the day-to-day operation of the business and more involved in administration. Armando's responsibilities grew as he rebuilt our facilities due to hurricane damage. The transition was from thatched teepees with a common bathhouse to raised romantic palapas with large rooms, shaded porches and private baths with hot water. He had much more to maintain when rebuilding was completed.

Eventually, I needed to stay in Carrillo to oversee the office and I adapted to town life by allowing frequent visits to the beach. During a recent enforced absence I had from Mexico due to illness, Armando needed an absorbing project. He found it by building a new home for us, though he says it is for me. In Carrillo Puerto, he created a house and garden with a large oval swimming pool. It is his pride and joy; however, there was not any place that I could be alone to scribble the closing of this book. I suggested that he design and build a studio just for me, and that is where I am: in a third floor Maya garret struggling to convey my gratitude to be able to keep my pen moving in this great life.

Armando (and Sonja) accepting the first prize at a tournament in Cozumel—a pick up truck as well as many other prizes!

INDEX

BIOGRAPHIES

SONJA LILLVIK

Photo by Sarah Craige

When Sonja Lillvik first encountered the Maya world, the meeting occurred in a kitchen. Hired as a manager at Kai Lu'um, a rustic but elegant resort on the Maya Caribbean, Sonja arrived without forewarning that her staff consisted of mostly monolingual Maya speakers. With cooking as the medium of communication, Sonja rose to the challenge and learned to create regional gourmet meals. Increasingly intrigued by Maya culture, Sonja soon sought further adventures in language and learning, a quest that brought her to Punta Allen, a lobster fishing village deep within the Mexican biosphere reserve called Sian Ka'an, in Maya, "the land where the sky was born."

Sonja Lillvik combines the organizational skills of the executive, the generosity of the teacher and the aesthetic sense of the artist with a keen spirit of adventure. Founder of a successful business in the San Francisco Bay area, Sonja conducted seminars to share her expertise with aspiring small business owners. Formerly an assistant clinical professor at the University of California, she pursued her creative interests as a ceramic artist and gourmet cook. She explored the intricacies of Middle Eastern, Korean, Japanese and French cuisine. Skiing, scuba diving, and flying airplanes nourished the love of adventure, which later led her to the Yucatán peninsula.

There, through the universal language of food, Sonja found herself drawn even deeper into the daily rituals of Maya life. To share her appreciation of this culture and cuisine, Sonja founded Cuzan Guest House with her husband, Armando Lopez, a Maya lobster fisherman. Located in Punta Allen, a fishing village in Sian Ka'an Biosphere Reserve, Casa Cuzan has provided a center for cultural exchange in a community otherwise remote from the outside world.

The first in the area to embrace eco-tourism, Sonja and Armando sponsor activities which introduce visitors to the beauties of the biosphere, while offering local residents both new skills and new applications of native wisdom (they have hosted groups from Earth Watch and from universities, involving foreign and native scholars in a shared learning environment). Functioning also as a fishing lodge, Casa Cuzan employs native guides who draw on their knowledge of the waters of Ascension Bay to locate the bonefish, tarpon and snook sought by fly fishermen from all over the world. Each year, Sonja and Armando organize a sports fishing tournament at Cuzan, drawing boats from Cozumel, Playa del Carmen, and other parts of the Caribbean coast. A major celebration featuring music, dance and festive foods, the tournament benefits the Punta Allen schools.

In a new venture, Sonja and Armando turn their attention from the coast to develop an inland nature preserve, Rancho el Angel. Here visitors traverse wooded paths beneath a forest canopy adorned with orchids, butterflies and tropical birds, while a Maya guide shares lore from medicinal plants to local legends. A feast from Armando's open hearth completes the experience. At sylvan Rancho el Angel, as at Casa Cuzan on the Caribbean, Sonja and Armando link others with the Maya community through exploration, education and fine food.

DONNA NEILSON

Donna Neilson has been a constant support for the defining, refining and testing of the recipes for this book. She is a native Californian and world traveler who began to cook at a very early age. We made acquaintance through a Dutch connection. Soon I enjoyed Napa Valley feasts served in meadows, farmhouses and vineyards by Donna, her family members and hippie maidens wearing long dresses. It was the early seventies and eating and feasting great food was a pastime included in any gathering, be it an anti war march, rock concert or Thanksgiving. For a few years, Donna ran the Cuzan restaurant kitchen during high season. The result was high quality food as she grasped the importance of using regional ingredients and traditional recipes, which she adapted to please the palates of our guests. Back in the states in the cookbook world, she was known as one who could "read" and critique a recipe without even cooking it. In between cooking at fine northern California restaurants or catering companies, she found ingredients essential to our recipes and tested every one in her own well-stocked kitchen in Sonoma County. She also compiled a list of wines compatible with Maya meals and I always look forward to our get-togethers when visiting California. Her contribution to this book is enormous.

CAROL AMORUSO

Carol Amoruso was an early contributor to the project, working with and learning from traditional home and professional cooks in Felipe Carillo Puerto and Punta Allen. Carol assisted from a love of both the Yucatán and its cuisine. An inveterate traveler, she returns to the peninsula at least once a year. Carol has written extensively about travel and food for publications such as SheNetworks, Global Rhythm, and The Weekly as a journalist for over twenty years. Her cookbook credits include the translation, from Italian to English, of "Sophia Loren's Recipes and Memories," and she has recently colaborated with Pierre Thiam on "Yolele: Recipes from the Heart of Senegal."

Currently, Carol writes for and edits The Hispanic-American Village, a web page covering the Latino community in the U.S.

ORDER

The Painted Fish and other Mayan Feasts

at

order@cuzanpress.com

and visit

www.cuzanpress.com

www.thepaintedfish.com

VISIT

Cuzan Guest Hóuse

www.cuzanguesthouse.com

reservations@cuzanguesthouse.com